# What the Man in the Moon Told Me

## By Frank Stanton

*For anyone suffering from mental illness*
*and for all those who care for them*

# Foreword

This book is not the story of my whole life. Instead, it's a slice of what has otherwise been a full and enjoyable life. In 1998 I was diagnosed with bipolar disorder. While it has never defined me, it has colored a number of my experiences, and I see in retrospect it was doing so long before 1998. I attempt here to give an accounting of some of these experiences as well as a few others that I suspect may be associated with the illness.

I am fortunate to be able to say that my illness tends toward the milder end of the bipolar spectrum. This has allowed me to hold a regular professional job and to be both a husband and a father. Not everyone with bipolar disorder can say that. This bit of good luck, though, almost caused me to abandon the idea of writing this book. Would a high functioning person with bipolar disorder have anything of interest or value to contribute on the subject? And would the comparatively low hurdles that I have had to clear along my own path trivialize an illness that continues to cause so much suffering for countless others?

In the end, I decided that there are lessons to be learned

from each of our journeys, the small and the large. Wisdom is usually hard-earned and none of it is without value. Whether that is true or not and whether the telling of my story has been a worthwhile endeavor are judgments I leave to you, the reader.

When I am not nuts, which is most of the time, I am quite normal…or so it seems to me. It would probably shock the majority of my friends and co-workers to discover I have any personal experience with mental illness. Because of this, I have decided to change the names of the people (including myself) and many of the places described in the book in order to protect the privacy of all involved. Some would call this cowardice. So be it. It is also important to note that certain details and specifics of the timeline I have presented may be remembered differently by some of the people involved. This could not be helped. Neither manic nor depressed memories are entirely reliable. Their fallibility lies in the fact that at the time the memories were being made the mind responsible for doing so was, by definition, impaired. This makes later recollection of those strange and scattered memories a bit like trying to figure out what happened to a downed airliner by reconstructing the crash debris. In some instances the best you can hope for is "pretty close."

I hope if anyone reading my story has also been diagnosed with bipolar disorder and you see a bit of yourself in these pages, you will be comforted by the knowledge that you are not alone. You and I are both in some fine company. I hope that if it is a bipolar friend or family member you are trying to understand better, then my story will shed at least a weak light on why we sometimes do the things we do. For anyone simply curious about the disorder, I hope the fragments of knowledge I have gained through the years and my explanations of them will prove helpful to you.

# Contents

# Chapter 1

# Hitting Bottom

It feels strange being the passenger in my own car, seeing things from this perspective, but I am not driving today. My wife, Faith, is driving and we are on our way to the hospital. Later this afternoon she will drive herself back home. I will be staying.

I am not injured or physically ill. I am, however, crazy and this is unfortunate. It is unfortunate because I have about a million things in my life right now that require my attention. They will not be getting it.

I am not "think I am Jesus" crazy, or "wearing a tin foil hat" crazy, and that's something I suppose. What I am is bipolar, more specifically Bipolar II which is a slightly milder form of the illness than Bipolar I, although at this moment, the difference between the two seems an exercise in hair splitting. Bipolar disorder is a condition that causes abnormal shifts in mood from very high to very low. Either extreme can, at times, make it impossible to think, reason, or function normally.

In my most recent incarnation I am depressed, severely so, and for that matter, mildly psychotically so. My psychiatrist has determined that I am an imminent danger to myself. Cringe. She has ordered me at once to the hospital for inpatient treatment and stabilization. Not my proudest moment...if I were keeping track of such things.

My face feels, and I'm sure looks, as though it has been whittled out of wood. It has lost its ability to form expressions. As I no longer have any emotions, not having any facial expressions has so far not been problematic.

Faith and I do not speak. I see her in my peripheral vision. She turns to glance at me every so often. There is sadness and concern on her face. Disappointment is there too. Not for the first time with this illness, I feel hot shame.

I am letting her down. I know this. Neither of us needs to say it. The roles in our marriage were defined long ago and there was never any ambiguity in them. I am the rescuer and she is the rescued. It is my job to look after her. I am not doing my job.

She is not the only one I am letting down. I am letting down my kids, my co-workers, my friends, and everyone else who depends on me…everyone else who assumes, quite reasonably, that I am strong enough and capable enough to manage the simple business of my own life. I have failed everyone.

I try to apologize to Faith. I try to explain. I tell her about the spirit of my dead lover from another lifetime who whispers in my ear that she is waiting for me. I tell her about the prophetic things revealed to me by the man in the moon.

She is not getting it. She doesn't understand. I give up. I lean my head against the cool glass of the window and watch the world flash by seeing none of it.

We pull in to the valet at the hospital's entrance and get out. A lifetime ago I worked here as a nurse. This will be the first time I am here as a patient. I should be concerned that I will see someone I know who will try to speak to me, ask me why I'm here. I am not concerned about this or anything else. I am nothing at all. It's as if everything that was me has been removed, scraped out of me, all of it pulled out of my nose by a hook like one of those Egyptian mummies. From a distance I look like a person but when you come closer you see I am only a husk, dead on my feet.

Psychiatry is located on the fourth floor of the hospital. It is a locked unit. I remember the jokes from when I worked here before. 'This job is driving me crazy. I'm going to wind up on the fourth floor." "That guy is nuts. He belongs on the fourth floor." We step onto one of the elevators near the gift shop. As the doors close, Faith reaches out for the panel of buttons. She presses the four. I sigh.

Outside of the entrance to the psych unit, Faith uses an intercom to inform the nurses' station who we are and why we are here. It seems they have been expecting me and buzz us in. The small duffel bag I have brought with me is confiscated at once.

A nurse with a keen eye looks me over. She lifts my shirt to make sure I am not wearing a belt and instructs me to remove my shoe laces. Then she searches my duffle bag and removes anything I could use to hurt myself. She looks for all the obvious things such as glass bottles, drawstrings, and razors.

I don't have much, but she takes away a few of my things anyway including, inexplicably, my contact lens solution. I wonder idly if I will be deloused later.

Relived now of everything that I cannot be trusted with, I am led by a male nurse tech into a large day room with greenhouse style windows down one side. We sit down at a table. It feels like a such a relief, as if I've been on my feet for days, but all I have done is walk through the front door and ride up in the elevator. The tech is a big dude. Probably a job requirement around here for when things get sketchy. I think he explains what is going to happen but I can't be sure. It is difficult to hear him over the static in my head.

He keeps his voice soft, calming. My posture is probably giving away the growing urge I have to bolt. If I had the energy to bolt that is…which I don't.

He says there is some paperwork I need to fill out. When he sees the flash of panic in my eyes that this causes, he adds that a nurse will be helping me with it. I am overwhelmed by the enormity of completing any task at all right now. How can I fill out paperwork? I don't know anything. Are there lots of papers? When do I have to have them done by? The giant tech doesn't seem concerned. He gives me a reassuring smile, stands, and walks away, or vanishes.

In addition to a number of other tables like the one I am sitting at, there is a couch, a half dozen armchairs, as many recliners, two TVs and a small baby grand piano. The piano seems out of place here like it just wandered in by mistake, looked around in confusion, and sat down glumly in a corner. Even the furniture here is depressed.

After an indeterminate amount of time, an intake nurse sits down across the table from Faith and me and goes over a stack of paperwork, presumably the stack the tech had been referring to. She asks questions and collects our signatures where they are required. Faith does the talking and I let her. I feel like I'm disappearing.

I can see the nurse's lips moving and hear the timbre of her voice, but I'm not able to make sense of her speech. I wring my hands, turn away, and stare off into the distance. What's happening to me? Am I really being admitted to a locked psych unit? How did this happen? How did it get this bad? But then I suppose I know how. I know exactly how.

## Chapter 2

# New Shoes

I am ten years old and standing in the kitchen of my parents' house watching my mother cook dinner. I am in the sixth grade and have recently been discovering the connection that exists between clothing and a person's social status in school. No longer can I wear, without consideration, whatever I received for Christmas last year. Cliques are forming fast, reputations are being forged, and judgments are being made. In short, the pecking order which will stand for the next seven years until I graduate from high school is being determined now. Everyone is scrambling, trying to do all the right things, trying to hang out with all the right people. Time is running out and we all want to have a seat at the popular table when the music stops.

This year the "must have" shoe is a brown suede clunker made by Kinney's Shoes, The Great American Shoe Store. As is often the case with fashion, appearance is irrelevant, which is a good thing considering these shoes could not be uglier. The fact that they are also so heavy they would knock a person unconscious if a pair were to fall on them...is equally irrelevant. Like everyone else, I ignore my common sense and decide that I must have a pair of these leaden shoes or be left behind. All the cool people are already wearing them. I choose tonight to try my luck and ask for a pair.

I lean nonchalantly on the counter near my mother and ask, "Mom, can I have some new shoes?"

She is standing in front of the stove adjusting the flame beneath a pot. I have no idea what she is cooking but it smells amazing. Something perhaps that began with sautéed onions I think. My mother is British and cooks staple foods...meat and potatoes. Her meals are always tasty and satisfying. Like most kids, I think my mother is the greatest cook in the world. I love to loiter around the kitchen when she is cooking, peeking under pot lids and sipping samples off spoons that she holds out to me.

She turns at my question to peer at me through a pair of large glasses with red plastic rims. She has a pleasant face and wears her hair in typical "mom cut." She looks every bit the librarian that she is. Nodding toward my feet she asks, "Have you already outgrown those?"

"Not really," I say honestly. "But these are just sneakers. I was wondering if I could get of pair of nicer shoes to wear at school and stuff."

She raises her eyebrows at me. I have never wanted to wear anything else *but* sneakers.

"Everyone is wearing these brown suede shoes from Kinney's."

"Mmmm," she says noncommittally and returns her attention to the bubbling pot in front of her. She shakes in some spice from a tiny rectangular tin and stirs it in with an old wooden spoon. The spoon was once light brown but has turned dark with years of use. There is a burn spot on the handle. I wait.

After a minute she says, "Well, I suppose I didn't get you any shoes this year with your school clothes. Are you sure those are the ones you want?"

"I'm sure," I say. Then hesitating, "Can we get them tonight?"

She sighs. I am pushing it I know, but nothing ventured and all that.

She considers it then says, "I don't want to go out anymore tonight. See if your father will take you. I think he has to pick something up at the auto parts store."

Oooh. I didn't count on this. Now I must weigh my desire to wear a pair of new reputation-making shoes to school tomorrow against the awkwardness of accompanying my father to the store to buy them. A tough call indeed.

## Chapter 3

# Living On Eggshells

My father is a difficult man on a good day. He is brilliant but volatile. A top-level aerospace engineer who it seems to me is pushed to the limits of his very scant patience each day by his job. He comes home most nights tired, edgy, and ready for a fight. Without saying as much, he dares anyone in the house to say the wrong thing to him, which is anything at all, or to look at him the wrong way, which is any way at all, so that he can then rip them to pieces. My mother, sister, and I are the outlet on which he vents his anger.

He is never physically abusive but his temper is so fierce that whoever he turns it on is left shattered and usually in tears. We have all been treated to the experience enough times to fear it. No one is safe, not even my mother, though she fares better than either my sister or me.

My sister Celia is a year older than I am and, like me, was adopted. Our parents were unable to have children of their own due to medical issues. Sometimes I wonder if my father wanted kids at all or just agreed to adopt in order to please my mother. Whatever the reason was, it seems to me to be his biggest regret. Celia and I stay permanently on his last nerve. As a consequence, the two of us slink around him most of the time like nervous puppies, our eyes downcast hoping to go unnoticed.

My father is not without his moments. On rare occasions he talks kindly to me and seems interested in the things I am doing. There was a time when I was lured in by these calms in his otherwise stormy demeanor. With the innocence of the child I was, I would start to believe that maybe he didn't hate me after all. Maybe he saw something in me he might even like. Inevitably though, when I was least expecting it, he would turn on me like a pit bull. It was just his nature.

The attack, when it came, and it always came, may have only been verbal but was no less devastating for that mercy. He would shred me to the bone over some silly point he thought worth driving home, yelling at me with wide flashing eyes and raised eyebrows. He would lean toward me, his self-control seeming to totter on the brink of violence. Any attempt to defend myself against the onslaught would only make things worse.

I have a distinct memory of cowering in front of my father once when I was maybe five years old. My family was about to leave the house and I had put my shoes on the wrong feet. My father took one look at them and barked at me that the buckle was supposed to be on the inside. I had no idea what he was talking about. I was wearing lace-ups. My confusion set off his highly combustible temper. "The buckle goes on the inside!" he shouted. Then when I made no move to correct my mistake, he shouted again, then again till he was raging and red-faced. Over and over. Always the same nonsensical statement never varying, demanding that I get it simply because he was saying it louder. I didn't get it. I didn't have any buckles. I kept picturing those black shoes the Pilgrims wore. Tears began to roll down my cheeks as I stared helplessly at my feet because I had no idea how to make my father stop shouting at me. I was terrified, frustrated, and bewildered. Celia finally came to my rescue figuring out that my shoes were on the wrong feet and helping me to switch them.

It would be nearly 35 years when talking about a piece of wood that had buckled due to water damage that I would realize what my father had been saying all those years ago. Buckle is a synonym for curve. The curve of the shoe goes to the inside. Ahhh.

Growing up, these all too frequent occurrences would leave my nerves in tatters. Feeling angry and impotent, I would hate myself for my vulnerability and vow never to open up again, never to let myself get close to him, but I did. I did far too many times. Finally the day came though that I just couldn't anymore.

Now I am skittish and guarded around my father at all times. Words with us are rare, conversations nonexistent. It is a new paradigm that has developed between the two of us, one that will remain in place for long years to come. When we are forced to speak to one another, only the most essential details are communicated. No frills under this new system and it suits both of us just fine.

Those interactions that are unavoidable are almost all carried out in the same fashion, him to me. Instructions given out and followed without question. "Hand me that screwdriver." "Turn that off." "Pass the mashed potatoes." I get the feeling that this is how he likes it. He is all business. I have become what he wants, a child seen but not heard, and increasingly, not seen either. It took him some years of work but he has finally broken me.

In time I will realize that my younger self was too hard on my father. Despite his ferocious temper and penchant for yelling, he was solid, consistent, responsible, and fearless. Not having a selfish bone in his body, he always took care of his family before himself and was reliable as the sun.

At ten years old, however, I do not yet have the perspective required to appreciate my father's strength of character. My perceptions of him are a child's perceptions. All I know at this point is that I am afraid of him and that we don't like each other very much. The idea of him taking me to buy a pair of shoes, just the two of us, is about as appealing as being clubbed unconscious by a dude wielding a can of beans in a pillowcase. In the end, though, I agree to do it. I really need those shoes.

## Chapter 4

# Ugly

There is not a Kinney's in my hometown of Gulfview, Texas, so we have to drive to the neighboring town of Bayshore to get the shoes. This means a twenty minute drive alone in the car with my father. Not pleasant. Neither of us speaks and my father never plays the radio. He dislikes noise of any kind. I stare out the window and ignore the tension that hovers around him perpetually like a swarm of angry bees and he likewise ignores me.

When we arrive, I follow him silently into the store and go to look for the shoes that I hope will springboard me to sixth grade cooldom. Without them, my spiraling social descent is guaranteed. Shoes make the man, right?

A few minutes after my father and I enter the store, two girls maybe a year or so older than I am come in with a woman. I have never seen the girls before and guess they probably go to school in Bayshore. Both of them I notice are very pretty. Unfortunately they have reached the age where they know that they are pretty and know that this makes them better than other people. By other people, I of course, mean ugly people. And by ugly people, I of course, mean me.

While the woman walks away to browse on her own, the two girls begin to wander around the store. They chat and gossip trailing their fingers over an occasional shoe as they pass. They don't seem to be shopping themselves, just killing time while they wait for the woman who I assume is the mother of one of them.

My father and I by this time are sitting on a bench near the back of the store. A salesman with his sleeves rolled up to the elbows is fitting me for a pair of the clunkers. After he helps me into them and laces them up, he has me stand. He mashes on the end of the shoe with his thumb. He has me walk up and down the aisle. I feel like I have a couple of boat anchors tied onto my feet.

"They feel good," I lie when he asks me what I think.

I'm not watching the two pretty girls yet I know exactly where they are at all times. It's like a sixth sense. I guess guys of all ages have it. It's kind of uncanny. I use this sense to time my glance perfectly and look up "casually" just as the two girls come around a rack of shoes near us.

I will tell my friends about the girls tomorrow. I will tell them that they were foxes. I make eye contact for a fleeting instant with one of the girls and then look away again keeping my face expressionless and bored. Detachment is cool. Chicks dig that sort of thing.

The girls pass by and turn up the next aisle. As they do, I see from the corner of my eye that they turn and glance back at me. Clearly, their assessment of me is less flattering than mine of them because before they are tactfully out of earshot I hear them giggle. It is not a good giggle. It is a snicker.

I know well the sound of a snicker. I know it from my extensive experience of being snickered at, and the derision in it slaps me to my senses. I feel suddenly foolish for having looked at them. I should know better. I tried to look casual but girls know when they're being checked out. They have a sixth sense too.

Their giggle is a sneering, "fat chance" or a, "please tell me you're kidding, right?" My face flushes and I pray silently that my father didn't hear it. Things like this should not surprise me any longer but they still do. I sometimes just forget that I am, and this is putting it kindly, a peculiar looking kid. I know then and there that it is going to take more than this pair of shoes to change what I am. Let me explain.

My parents are not poor. We are a comfortable middle class family. This does not prevent my parents, however, from being cheap. They are not cheap with everything, but certainly with a majority of things and my haircuts are among them.

Once every month and a half or so I am taken to a barber college 40 minutes from our house. There, a cosmetology student gets to practice on me and I get a cut rate hair cut from them in return, or what passes for one. This is a win-win situation in my parents' estimation. Because of the length of time that passes between haircuts, my parents always ask that my hair be cut as short as possible so it will last until our next visit. This less-than-optimal grooming schedule leaves my hair almost always either too short or too long.

Tonight as I stand in Kinney's trying on shoes, it is too short, hilariously too short. It is far shorter than the current style for kids my age and that's just for starters. Even if it were possible for a haircut like this to be overlooked by those girls, which it isn't, the rest of the package that is ten-year-old Frank Stanton would have been more than enough to coax a snicker from two pretty girls.

I am pale skinned, wear thick glasses, have severe buck-teeth, and spaghetti-thin arms. I have a "prominent" nose set on a head no bigger than a grapefruit, long gangly limbs, and big feet. These unfortunate attributes combine to form the perfect nerd-storm. Who wouldn't have laughed. I am a cartoon character.

I am so aware of my own ugliness that I have avoided looking in mirrors since around the age of eight and will continue to do so long into adulthood. I also flinch every time someone takes my picture, another habit that I will be unable to break.

My parents are frustrated to no end by this particular aversion because it has led me to throw away nearly every set of school pictures that I ever received. My teachers would hand them out for me to bring home and I would instead drop them discretely into the trash the first chance I got. I knew I would be yelled at by my parents because the pictures had already been paid for, but to me, it was always worth it.

The salesman with the rolled up sleeves helps me out of the shoes. He boxes them back up and hands them to my father. I follow my father to the front of the store where he pays for them at the register. As we are turning to leave, the girls make one more pass by us, a last look, a bit of fun to make themselves feel superior. I feel like an idiot and turn away from the grins that this time they do not even try to hide.

My face flushes so hard my ears feel hot. My father seems oblivious but I have a feeling he is only pretending to be. I wonder if I should apologize to him. I wonder if I should have prepared him better.

I have always been a sensitive child and will only manage to grow the thinnest of skins as an adult. My mother says that I just feel things more intensely than other children and that it's one of the things she loves about me. I don't love it.

I was an emotionally defenseless child and a cry baby growing up. My feelings were always so close to the surface and so easily hurt. I was and am a perfectionist and ruthlessly self-critical. I accept responsibility and blame for whatever goes sour and see it all as my fault. Ridicule, of which I receive plenty, strikes me like blows and stays with me leaving behind deep scars. It's a toxic brew of personality traits when considered along with the ticking genetic time bomb of bipolar disorder.

These qualities were probably inherited from one or both of my birth parents and don't pair well with my somewhat unfortunate grab bag of physical attributes. They might, however, help to explain why, as I leave Kinney's holding my absurdly heavy new shoes in a plastic bag, that the lump I feel in my throat is not for myself. I have been made fun already enough in my short life to have become accustomed to it. Tonight, though, it is my father that I feel sorry for.

A parent, I assume, always maintains a degree of prejudice on behalf of their child. I guess my father does for me too. I'm sure they can't help but see their child in a more flattering light than does the rest of the world. They must also hold, secreted away in their hearts, a treasure chest of private hopes for what their child will one day become.

When my parents brought me home as a baby my father must have imagined something *Leave it to Beaver*ish for me. He must have hoped, for example, that I would grow up to be a mischievous but well-mannered young boy who might throw newspapers for extra money. That later I would go on to play ball for my high school team and date a string of pretty girls. He must have hoped that I would attend my senior prom, would smile in pictures, would be well-liked and happy…that I would grow up to be the All-American boy. Even my father must have wanted that.

Before tonight, I think, he may not have realized how far short I would fall of those dreams. No one wants to find out that their kid is a nerd-storm. His eyes would be open now though. And although there is no love lost between us, I feel the pain of his loss or what I imagine is his loss. I have, by simply being me, ruined another of his dreams.

I already know what I am but he has only just found out. I wish I could say something to comfort him, be something more than what I am. As we climb back into the car to head home my eyes are moist because of the sadness and embarrassment I assume my father must be feeling. In my ten-year-old mind, I have hurt him. I am a disappointment. Again.

## Chapter 5

# Drowning

I am an embarrassingly melancholy teenager. It is the summer between my sophomore and junior years at Gulfview High School (Class of 1985) and I am incapable of enjoying almost any aspect of my life. It is a secret I hide from everyone I know.

I don't understand why I should feel any different from other kids my age but I'm not like them at all. My interest in sports, car engines, drinking, or listening to loud rock music barely registers when compared to my friends. Everyone is unique and at our age we're all living in a bath of hormones. Maybe I shouldn't be concerned if I'm a little more despondent than my peers. It's adolescence, right?

I suppose, for a lucky and well-adjusted few, high school is shaping up to be the best years of their lives. Kudos to them. I think of them as the swimmers. They not only swim but they backstroke their way through high school with infuriating ease, playfully spewing a fountain of water from their lips. There are more than enough of these kids around to annoy the crap out of me but they do not make up the majority. There are plenty of others too.

There are the kids that, like the backstrokers, manage to swim their way through high school, but for them, it requires some real effort. They're making it but not winning any trophies along the way. There are the dog paddlers. They make it any way they can and you have to respect them for their perseverance if for nothing else.

At the other end of the scale, where I live, there are the drowners. These kids can be further divided into two subsets. Those in subset A don't even try to swim. They already know that all is lost and give up without a fight. They sink like a sack of anvils and couldn't care less. Those in subset B know they don't have a prayer of making it either but can't seem to help from thrashing and flailing in a panic as they try to keep their heads above water…for all the good it does them. In the end, they go down just as surely as those subset A.

I belong to subset B but would trade up to A if I could. There must, I suspect, at least be some solace found in giving up. I could stop fighting, stop beating myself up. I could let go of caring what happens or what people will think of me if I fail. I could let go of this whole stinking system. I'm never going to fit into it anyway. I could just sink away into the darkness. Too dramatic? Yeah, I suppose it is. Scratch that.

We drowners entertain no such foolish ideas that high school will be the best years of our lives. Oh God, please don't let these be the best years of my life. We write off our time in high school as unrecoverable.

We don't buy class rings, we don't buy yearbooks, and we will never, even under the threat of death, return for a reunion. We want no memories of these four years. I am a drowner through and through, and if I could I would take high school and shove it up the asses of all those back stroking pricks. I am miserable.

I have a best friend, Brian. I'm sure like most kids our age, he is probably navigating through his own private struggles, but to me, he seems to be everything I am not. Because of this I try to be better so that I will deserve his friendship. When we hang out, he listens and he talks and for reasons utterly beyond my comprehension, he values my opinions. He makes me laugh, usually hysterically until I can't breathe, and is surely the only reason that I do, in fact, against all odds make it.

I hide, or try to hide my darker side from Brian. It is not all right for boys my age to be melodramatic, sad, hopeless, or otherwise despairing. Society is clear on these points and the price for ignoring them is steep. So I do what everybody does. I compartmentalize my feelings. I fake it. I do whatever I have to do to cram my square peg personality into the round hole that society demands I do if I ever want a shot at acceptance. Ultimately, of course, I fail...but not straight away.

At 15 I am not an obvious trainwreck of a kid and we have a few of those at my school so I know what I'm talking about. I am pretty good at keeping all my unacceptable bits corralled within the walls of my bedroom at home. There, however, hidden from judgmental eyes, I lay exhausted on my bed wondering why everything feels so difficult. Hating myself has become a hobby and one I am good at. I loathe myself like some people knit sweaters or play the guitar.

I listen to terribly depressing music because I relate to the lyrics. I read...a lot. With a librarian for a mother, I have grown up in libraries and bookstores spending countless hours lost between the pages of books. I find escape and countless kindred souls within the pages of books. I lean unsurprisingly toward gloomy classics such as *The Catcher in the Rye*, *The Great Gatsby*, *Wuthering Heights*, and *David Copperfield*.

I discover poetry and read it like a dirty little secret. It moves me in ways not even books manage to. I write some of my own, too, for the guilty catharsis in it. I think it may be pretty good, but I always throw it away afterwards. Too revealing.

I spend hours drawing, a talent that, according to the scant history given to my parents by the orphanage, I inherited from my biologic mother. Some nights I sit at the desk in my room drawing by lamp light into the early morning hours. During these precious times, I lose all track of time and place. The house is quiet, everyone sleeping but me. The smells of wood pencil shavings and graphite scent the air around me.

Something drives me to create, to capture the impermanent beauty and poignancy I see in the world. I want people to see my art and be unable to take their eyes from it. I want to move them to their bones, to haunt them. I want to bring goose bumps to their skin and tears to their eyes. I want to inspire them and break their hearts. If I succeed, they may begin to see the world the way I see it and in doing so, they just might see me too.

People are my favorite subject to draw. Like Edgar Degas, I love to draw ballet dancers. It is more than just the female form. It is something about the sacrifice dancers make for their art. Their physical beauty is more captivating because it is colored by obsession. One that goes undampened by the requisite physical suffering that dance almost always demands so much. The passion-fueled drive to accomplish greatness always captures my interest. I draw athletes for the same reason, animals for their simplicity and innocence, and the weathered faces of old people for their character.

It's not always a higher form of art that I try to create. Sometimes I draw beautiful women with impossibly large breasts. I am, after all, 15. And sometimes I draw my own comics. The comics, not uncommonly, contain themes of death and suicide and like the poetry, I always throw those away when I am finished.

When I at last snap off the lamp and crawl into my squeaky bed with the ancient metal box springs, I lay in the dark and think up stories in my head. I am the central character and the central character always dies. As I close my eyes and sleep overtakes me, I pretend it is death. I pretend I will not have to wake up in the morning, or comfortingly, ever again. Sometimes I pretend people will care.

With the passing of years I find the inexplicable pall of sadness that hangs over me becoming more episodic. Which is to say that it occasionally recedes for a while and allows me to breathe. During these times I laugh with my friends, complete my school assignments, watch TV, and when I am lucky, spend the night at Brian's house. I never have to fake being a normal teenager at these times. I am one. But when my respite is over and the gloom settles back over me like the rain over Seattle, it feels colder, wetter, and more miserable than ever.

I once heard that when backpackers sit down to rest, they should not remove their packs because the packs will feel heavier when it comes time to put them back on. I don't know if it's true, but I can understand the reasoning. The load is easier to shoulder if you are already accustomed to its weight. A rest sometimes just makes things worse.

The predictable return of my low mood is getting to be as familiar as it is unpleasant. It makes me feel discouraged and separated from my friends. They seem to be managing a more even keeled adolescence, but who knows. Maybe they're just hiding it better. My own emotional desolation is getting harder to keep confined to my bedroom. Wisps of it are curling out from under my door like smoke and the rest of the household is starting to notice.

## Chapter 6

# Is There Something We Should Know?

I come downstairs on a Saturday morning to get a bowl of cereal. My mother is sitting at the table in front of a half-finished cup of tea and the morning paper. A ghostly twist of steam rises from her cup. The tea is made English style, with milk and sugar, the way she always drinks it. The paper is in disarray and there is a small plate with a sprinkling of toast crumbs on it that has been pushed to one side. She stops reading and looks up when I enter the room. I feel her eyes follow me as I take down a bowl and fill it with some Cheerios from the pantry.

My parents buy only three brands of cereal while my sister and I are growing up: Corn Flakes, Rice Krispies, and Cheerios. These alone pass their muster. The rest are junk, sugary children's cereals that will rot the teeth right out of our heads. They alternate the cereals, buying them in rotation so that we don't get tired of them. It doesn't work. I'd shave off my eyebrows for a bowl of Fruit Loops or Lucky Charms.

After splashing some milk over my Cheerios I carry them to the table and sit down across from my mother. Without a word I begin spooning them into my mouth exasperated by the effort that it requires.

"Are you on drugs?" my mother asks me. This is how she initiates conversation these days. She studies me with an uncomfortable intensity.

I don't look up. "What?" I say, even though I heard her. I force another spoonful of the loathsome little O's into my mouth. My voice is a murmur, barely audible, but I don't care. I don't feel like having this conversation again, or any conversation for that matter. I feel like closing myself up in a dark closet and going to sleep behind the coats.

"You heard me," she says. "Are you doing drugs?"

"No, Mom." I sigh. "Why do you always me ask that?"

"Well, you're always moping around here now and you hardly ever talk. They say those are signs."

"Who says?"

"People. Parents who found out their teenagers were doing drugs. That's who."

I just resist rolling my eyes. My parents have threatened me within an inch of my life for eye rolling. It sets them off faster than just about anything.

"Well, I'm not doing drugs," I mumble. "I don't even know anyone who does drugs." And it's true, I don't. Finally I glance up at her and meet her gaze. I can tell this is important to her. "Mom, seriously, I'm not. Okay."

"Is anything else the matter then? You just don't seem happy anymore." Her eyes bore into me.

"I'm fine, Mom. I'm just tired."

She exhales through her nose. Then she nods and lets it go for now. She will bring it up again though. She always does. I wonder what kinds of conversations go on about me behind the closed door of my parents' bedroom at night. They know that I don't fit in, that I'm not like other teens. Like me, they worry that something may be wrong but none of us knows what it might be.

I want to tell her, I'm not on drugs. I'm just miserable and I don't know why. I know I mope around all the time but I can't help it. I want to tell her that sometimes I think I may be losing my mind because there's nothing wrong with my life and yet half the time I wish I was dead. And if this is what drugs make you feel like then why in God's name would anyone take them in the first place?

I don't say these things, of course. We don't have that kind of relationship. Instead, my mother returns to her paper and me to my cereal. When I am done I rinse my bowl, put it in the dishwasher, and trudge back upstairs to my room. It's not even 9:00 in the morning and I am exhausted. I climb back into bed and close my eyes. I do not get up again until late in the afternoon.

This summer I am working as a janitor at the library where my mother works. She got me the job. It's a little embarrassing knowing that the only reason I was hired was because of my mother's position there, because I'm still a year shy of the legal working age. I don't complain. I know I am lucky to have a job at all.

I work just 25 hours a week, from 7 a.m. till noon

Monday through Friday and have the afternoons off. It's a good gig, though like everything else in my life, it feels like a grueling soul-withering chore that requires a titanic effort to complete each day.

It is almost unbearably hot this summer. The air is thick and tropical, like breathing steam, and the cicadas buzz ceaselessly in the trees all day. I can't even remember what a breeze feels like. Everyday I ride my bike the three or so miles to work and arrive drenched in sweat. I let myself in with a key and turn on the lights.

If I appreciate anything at all about the job it is this time of the day, the first two hours before the library opens to the public and I am alone. There is no one around to require anything of me. No one around to whom I might be expected to speak. I push the vacuum cleaner up and down between the shelves of books as early morning sun spills in through the high windows catching dust motes in its light.

I love the friendly smell of so many books. All libraries smell this way…comforting. Sometimes it is in these times, however, I find that without warning, I am no longer in the library at all. I am in my bed and it is the middle of the night. Not my bed at home but another bed somewhere in a Dickensesque England. Maybe I'm in London, sometime well before the turn of the century. I don't know for sure but I've been here plenty of times before. Stay with me now. Things are about to get a little strange.

# Chapter 7

# 3:00 a.m.

There is snow on the ground outside and on the sill of my drafty second story window. The floor and ceilings are bare timbers and the walls are dirty plaster. I sit up and swing my feet over the side of the bed. I like this place. It is my home. I know that much. The floor is ice cold on my bare feet so I stuff them into the slippers that sit next to the bed. They are equally cold but at least they're soft.

I stand up and walk across the darkened room to the window. It's so cold in here that I can see my breath. Moonlight sparkles off the frost that has formed on the rippled panes of glass. I should really get some curtains. I have no idea what time it is. I have no clock of my own. They are too expensive. I haven't heard the big bell in the tower clock for a long time and I can't see its dimly illuminated face from this, my only window. Still, I'm guessing it must be around 3:00 in the morning.

I look out over the city's empty streets and snowy rooftops. I see thin curls of smoke drift up from a dozen chimneys. My own fireplace is dark and long cold. Coal is not cheap either. I lay my palm against the glass, try to gauge how cold it is outside. A shiver runs through me and I take my hand away.

I look back at my bed in the corner. It's no more than a straw-filled mattress on a rough wooden frame strung with rope. The sheets are worn and smell like me. There is a me-sized imprint in the middle of the mattress where I sleep.

A small table sits next to the bed with a book, open and face down to save my page. The stub of a candle and a half-filled ceramic cup of water, probably near freezing, rest next to the book. A rickety wooden chair that needs a new straw seat leans against the wall at the foot of the bed. I can't sit on it anymore but it works well to drape my clothes over and which is, by the way, where my clothes are currently draped. My shoes are there too, on the floor where I left them last night and an empty chamber pot is just within reach under the bed.

I shuffle back over, kick off my slippers and climb in, settling on my side into the still warm groove there. I pull the sheet, thick wool blanket, and quilt up over my head. I leave a tiny hole to breathe through like a seal under the ice. Then somewhere in the distant night I hear the old tower clock ring out. Three mournful bongs. Just like thought. I smile.

Then I'm back. The library again. This has been happening more and more, bouncing unexpectedly between the present and one of two different places in the past. This morning it was the "London" flat. The other, when I travel to it instead, is a field near a small creek. I am an Indian there.

I used to think it was all in my head but now I'm not so sure. An idea has taken root in my mind that maybe I exist simultaneously in three different places and three different times. I feel increasingly certain that wherever I spend the most time I will become the most real. In the others, I will fade away by an equal measure.

I have been nervously considering the implication of this hypothesis. If it is true then I may not have to stay here in this time and place. It may be that I can decide where and when I want to exist. I am unhappy here, it's true, but I know how to live here and what is expected of me. Realistically, how would I survive in another time and place? And if the "problems" I hope to escape from are really all on the inside, then won't I just be carrying them with me wherever I go? No. It seems safer, at least for the time being, to remain where I am.

The presence of my separate lives waiting to be lived does remain a comforting option for me, always available if I change my mind. It is a secret I keep and share with no one. It scares me a little because the places seem to have a sort of gravity to them. They tug at me if I am not fully engaged in the present.

I find myself drifting away sometimes even when I have no conscious intention to do so. Times like when I'm mowing the grass, or washing dishes, or like now when I'm vacuuming between the stacks in the library before the doors open. It just happens.

It is like living in the surf and constantly feeling the pull of an undertow. It is nice sometimes to let it take me out a little way, but if I ride it too far I worry I may not be able to get back in. I have to keep my wits about me.

I realize that the existence of alternate lives in alternate times may be in my head. It would make more sense if they were but that explanation disregards my personal experience. I don't ask Brian his opinion about it. I don't want him to think I'm crazy. He would definitely say it was in my head and then, I'm sure, question the wisdom of remaining friends with someone so obviously a loon. I can't blame him for that, but the seeing, touching, and smelling I experience are real. Because of them I have no choice but to accept what is happening to me regardless of the impossibility of such an occurrence.

Ultimately it is a question I do not need answered, a proof I do not require. Whatever it is, it is out of my hands. I acquiesce to it like I always do in my life. It is what it is. This ability to accept things, even things that are odd or unpleasant can be a valuable quality to have. Still, such a fragile grip on reality will cause problems for me in the years to come when my mind becomes truly sick.

# Chapter 8

# First Cut

Late one afternoon when I am home alone after work, I am laying on my bed. I have no desire to visit friends or watch TV or read. I have no desire at all. I am empty. My thoughts once again turn toward the idea of suicide. I know it makes no sense. I haven't a thing to complain about but that only makes it worse. Why can't I handle what everyone else my age is handling so easily? I would be humiliated by my weakness but no one knows about it. I could try to say it's because of my strict father, or my ugliness, or my social awkwardness but it would only make the whole thing more pathetic. I couldn't produce a real problem if I tried. And believe me, I've tried.

I wish there was something, anything to blame my unhappiness on other than what I know is the problem. It's me. I am defective, pathetic, someone not ready, unable to cope, unable to join in, hopelessly unprepared, an embarrassment, unneeded, unfit, and unwanted, even by me.

I wonder sometimes who up in heaven made the colossal

mistake of sending me down here to live when surely it had been so obvious that I was doomed to fail. Maybe there was a slip up somewhere. Some corner-cutter covering his ass. He had to get someone down here to fill a body and no one better was available. He knew I would be a disaster but it was me or no one and it simply couldn't be no one. Someone would have his job for that.

He must've shrugged his shoulders and figured, what the hell. He wished me luck, pulled the lever or whatever they do up there, and sent me in. I'd make it or I wouldn't but as far as he was concerned, problem solved. Nice. It was probably a Friday up in heaven when I was conceived, at 4:45 in the afternoon just before a long weekend.

I know good and well I have no reason to feel the way I do but that knowledge doesn't change it. I feel it anyway. Thank God I don't have to justify it to anyone because I can't. I'm tired of feeling, not just this but everything. I'm ashamed and so very sorry but this is just not working out. I'm miserable all the time and the sustained effort it takes to keep fooling all the people around me that I'm happy has taken everything I've got. I can't do it anymore. I have nothing left. I'm a complete fake and was never meant to be here. Being abandoned by my birth mother was only the first proof. I was a mistake.

Life is an impressively long affair. I feel sure that I should be pacing myself to go the distance but haven't been able to. I've been sprinting flat out for as long as I can remember and still can't even keep up with the stragglers. And we haven't even got to the tough part yet. This high school stretch should be gravy!

If it's all the same to everyone else, and I have no doubt that it is, I think I'm ready to just drop out of this race. This…life was a terrible idea from the start. I want it to be over. I want to be gone and quickly forgotten, like I never was.

I wonder idly how I would do it. It is not the first time I have explored this line of thinking. My options are not great. I do not have a stash of sleeping pills in my medicine cabinet or, in fact, a medicine cabinet. I do not have a gun. I also rule out the idea of drowning or falling to my death because I do not want to be scared when I die. Similarly, I rule out hanging because I do not trust my ability to tie an effective knot. I have read that a noose must be tied just right in order to break one's neck when it snaps taut, otherwise the person could wind up twisting for several long and painful minutes while they asphyxiate.

In time I'll discover, of course, that there are a million ways I could kill myself. I'll consider most of them in my lifetime, but the depressed brain is not known for its ability to think outside the box, so right now, to my addled mind, that just leaves cutting.

Can I do that? Do I want to die so badly that I could drag a blade across my skin, press it into the soft flesh of my wrists deep enough to do the job? Could I sever the veins and ligaments and anything else in the way till I find the artery and flay it open? I am unsure. But I decide that I need to find out.

I do not want to die today. My mind is just turning over

possibilities. It is important that I know whether or not wrist cutting is going to be an option for me. Suicide, after all, feels like an eventual inevitability. I should have a plan. That's important, right? Besides, it's the first thing that has made me want to get off this bed since I collapsed here. So five minutes later, I am seated at my desk with my arm on a towel palm up in my lap and our sharpest kitchen knife in my other hand.

I bring the blade down to the pale flesh of my wrist. I won't cut deep, I promise myself. I just want to see if I can cut at all. Then I think better of it and, just in case, turn my arm palm down and expose the top of my forearm instead. I don't want any accidents here. No drama, especially the sort that involves calling attention to myself and my growing fixation with suicide. This is just a dry run, a warm up.

I remember when I was eleven and received a Barlow pocket knife as a gift. I wondered how sharp it was so I gently ran my thumb across the blade. It stung like liquid fire and laid open the pad of my thumb. I snatched back my hand in shock and stared at it a moment as it began to bleed profusely. It was so unexpected that it took my mind a second to process what had actually happened. I never thought it would be that sharp. I felt like an idiot. Would this feel like that?

My heart begins to beat faster. I take a breath, press the knife against my skin and yank it across my forearm. Nothing. Wait. Nothing? I look carefully. No blood. I have not even broken the skin. It seems that sharp enough to dice onions and green peppers in the kitchen is not the same as sharp enough to split skin in your room, let alone arteries.

I gather my nerve and go at it again. It takes several tries, experimenting with increasing pressure and pull speed before finally blood begins to ooze up along the path of the blade in pitiful little beads. Each attempt exhausts me emotionally because I keep getting ready for pain. Afterwards, I have to work up the nerve all over again for the next pull. I wish I had my old Barlow knife. That could do the job but I had broken the blade about a year ago using it to loosen a screw. It now lies rusting in the bottom of my toolbox.

I am disgusted with myself. Wow. What a baby. How can I ever hope to sever anything deep or vital when I can barely even break my skin? I want to give up, consider it one more proof of what a monumental loser I am, when on a frustrated impulse, I take several angry hacks at my arm. All three cut deep enough that before I know what I have done, blood is running freely down my arm in dark rivulets and onto the towel.

I watch them in fascination for a long moment before at last I wrap the towel around my arm and hold pressure to it. Then something unexpected happens. A calm spreads over me. I feel it move through my arms and legs. It is a relaxation I have never felt before, a welcome heaviness. My heart slows and I let out a long breath. My mind, which has been so filled with the constant chatter of recrimination, worry, and self-loathing, goes at long last, silent. I am at peace.

* * *

What I don't know that afternoon is that somewhere between 11 and 28 percent of adolescents on any given day meet the criteria for major depression depending on which source you consult. It is also true that most cases of bipolar disorder first appear during a person's teens or twenties. At 15 my understanding of depression is extremely limited and bipolar disorder is not on my radar at all.

Like so many people, adults included, I believe that depression is synonymous with sadness. I also believe that it is the understandable result of tragic or otherwise difficult circumstances such as experiencing the death of a loved one, losing a job, or enduring extended suffering. Depression without a situational cause can only mean one thing—weakness.

The unfortunate truth is that while painful or unhappy circumstances and depression are often linked, their relationship is not exclusive. Which is to say that although tragedy can certainly trigger a depressive episode, often times depression will present and exist independently of any situational cause. Depression oversimplified is just an imbalance of the neurotransmitters in the brain that, among other things, regulate mood. While we can point to some triggers of this imbalance, others remain a mystery to us. Sometimes depression just is.

It affects people indiscriminately ignoring sex, age, socioeconomic conditions, and/or strength of character. When an adolescent experiences depression, however, the symptoms are not uncommonly mistaken for melodramatic teen angst, hormones, drugs, or some other reasonable but ultimately incorrect explanation for what is going on. This error sometimes comes at a price. Suicide is tragically the third leading cause of death in the U.S. for people between the ages of 15 and 24.

Self-harm is the intentional injury of one's own tissue without suicidal intent, most commonly as a means of coping with intense negative emotions such as depression, anxiety, and low self-esteem. It is usually, but not exclusively, seen in teens and young adults, but once a person has self-harmed it is more likely that they will return to the behavior again later in life during times of high stress. It is also interesting to note that while self-harm is a long acknowledged hallmark of borderline personality disorder, many studies actually find the incidence to be just as high among bipolars.

* * *

Over the next few weeks, I continue the cutting, first on one arm and then the other. No longer am I trying to see if I have the nerve to open the arteries in my wrists. I don't. I am now only after the peace that the cutting brings. Depression hurts. It has a quality of constant unendurability to it like walking around with thumbtacks in your shoes, only the thumbtacks are inside of you. You cannot take your mind from it and cannot remove the source of the pain.

It's exhausting and unrelenting. Everything is a chore

and you just want it to end. It doesn't occur to you that it is episodic and that it will pass like a bad cold if you can just hold on. It feels like the problem is life itself. It feels like it will never get any better and the only escape from it is through sleep or death. Now I have a new option, though. Cutting.

Cutting acts as an overflow valve that releases misery. The awfulness inside me continues to grow. I can't stop it. My mind is becoming polluted, churning and stinking with repetitive negative thoughts. Yet each time it reaches an unbearable level I can bleed off some of the excess with a few cuts. It provides a temporary rest. Makes me feel quiet inside and drowsy. Sometimes after I cut, I lay down on my bed and fall into a dreamless sleep. When I wake again I feel stronger. I tell myself I will carry on a while longer. You know, just see how it goes.

# Chapter 9

# Too Close For Comfort

My sister Celia and I have never been close. She and I are just too different from one another. Still, growing up together can create bonds between even the most unlikely individuals; sometimes bonds we don't even know are there. One afternoon I am walking into the kitchen and Celia passes me on her way out. She glances down at my arms as she goes by. She stops. I don't.

"Hey," she says.

I do not want to talk to her or anyone. "What?" I answer pulling open the door to the refrigerator.

She stands there, hesitates. Something is bothering her. "What happened to your arms?" Her voice is not curious. She is trying to make the question sound conversational but it isn't working. It is edged with something that makes us both uncomfortable. She is worried.

Why would she be worried? They're just cuts. She couldn't possibly guess that I was doing this to myself or for what purpose. Could she?

I am stunned. It is as if a glass of water has just been thrown in my face. How could I have been so stupid? Did I think no one would notice the damage I had been doing to myself? Did I think it just wasn't that obvious? No. I hadn't thought either of those things. I hadn't been thinking at all. I'd been walking around in a fog. Shit! My face flushes.

"Enhh, nothing," I say dismissively. I don't look at her. I pull out a jug of milk and turn my back to her letting the door close on its own. I set the milk on the counter and take down a glass from the cabinet. Please don't pursue this. Please don't pursue this. I keep my back to her.

"What did you do to them?"

Shit. I pour a glass of milk and return the jug to the refrigerator. "I scraped them." The cuts are superficial, all close to each other, and roughly parallel. I think they may resemble a bad scrape. Maybe they can pass. Celia watches me. I drink my milk down a little too fast and set the glass in the sink.

"They don't look like scrapes," she says.

"Yeah," I persist, breezing around her and heading back to my room. "I scraped 'em. They're fine though."

Hearing the uncharacteristic concern in my sister's voice wakes me up and makes me realize how closed in my thinking has been getting. How near I just came to discovery. As miserable as things seem to me right now I know they could be worse. It never even occurred to me that someone would notice what I was doing.

I consider my options. Wearing long sleeves all the time, especially in the summer, will raise too many questions, so a simple cover-up is not going to work. It seems as though all my young life I have been trying to fly below the radar. If no one notices me, no one will make fun of me. No one will see what a pathetic wash-out I am. I refuse to have my weakness put on display for everyone to see, so I shelve the whole technique for the time being and pray that the cuts I have already inflicted heal quickly before anyone else asks me about them.

* * *

I never cut myself on purpose again after that day. I wish I could say it was the last time I self-harmed at all but that, embarrassingly, would be a lie. In 1983 the term "cutter" had not yet, to my knowledge anyway, been coined. There was no Instagram or Twitter on the not-yet-existing Internet for kids to publicize their struggles. Neither were there any emo cliques at Gulfview...or for that matter, anywhere that I knew of. In fact, being troubled at all was not something anyone talked about.

Probably one of the reasons I didn't expect people to put two and two together if they noticed my cuts was that I wouldn't have. The cuts were on the top of my forearm, not my wrist, so it was obviously not a suicide attempt. And if they weren't a suicide attempt then weren't cuts just cuts? No cause for alarm. I had never heard of someone doing such a thing. I don't mean to imply that my difficulties or coping mechanisms were singular in nature, just that they seemed that way to me at the time.

Adolescence is a difficult time for a lot of kids so I cannot imagine that I was the only one handling my emotions in such an unhealthy manner. If anyone else was doing what I was doing, then like me, they were wisely keeping their behavior a secret. In hindsight, I must presume that disturbed kids have been harming themselves for long decades before I ever "discovered" it during my sophomore year of high school. We all stumbled upon it independently without instruction the same as we did with masturbation.

Cutting would not have met with even a fringe element acceptance in my high school. That sort of behavior would have been considered shocking and bizarre. The person harming themselves would have been branded a freak of the highest order, someone to be joked about behind their back and avoided at all costs. Discovery meant certain and permanent banishment from all high school social circles including my own. Why then would I risk it?

Self-harm has an addicting edge to it, as strange as that sounds. While it didn't make me feel good, it did stop me for a while from feeling bad. And like other addicts who lean on their vice of preference at different times for different reasons, so called "self-mutilators" (and for the record I hate that unnecessarily dramatic term) will cut or otherwise harm themselves for different reasons.

In the beginning, I did what I did to relieve the persistent and disturbing suicidal feelings I was experiencing. Soon, however, I found it was also excellent for guilt, frustration, and self-loathing which were other symptoms of my depression. It was a form of punishment, punishment I felt

I deserved, and once administered, brought me relief.

It went like this: I would become angry at myself for some unforgivable shortcoming such as being covered in acne or for my voice quavering like a little girl's while giving an oral report in front of the class, or for allowing myself to be bullied and not having the backbone to stand up for myself. A voice in my head, my Censor, would then berate me without mercy over the fact until I punished myself to its satisfaction. The worse the offense, the more cuts would be required. After it was done however, the voice would grow quiet again. I could continue eking by. And it worked. The self-loathing was the worst. At times it was so intense I was choking on it. It rose in the back of my throat like bile. I had to do something. In light of what nearly happened with my sister cutting was, thereafter, off my list of options. So where did that leave me?

# Chapter 10

# Ignition

It is evening, sometime in the weeks leading up to Christmas. My family and I have had our dinner and I have just finished clearing the table and washing the dishes. I think it would look cozy to light one of the cinnamon and apple scented candles that my mother liked around the holidays, and leave it burning in the center of the dining room table with the overhead light out. At 16 years old, match striking is still a new enough skill to fascinate me.

I light the candle and then stare at the still lit match as the flame creeps toward my fingers. I blow it out before it gets too close and a twist of fragrant gray smoke drifts up from it. I blow gently on the head of the spent match and am surprised to see it glow cherry red again. Then, on complete impulse, and for no reason I can think of, because it has been months since I hurt myself purposely, I press the glowing match to the inside of my forearm.

It burns. Shocker. I close my eyes though and hold it there for the three to five seconds it takes to stop burning.

When I pull it away and inspect the spot where it had been I see a tiny match head-sized divot where my skin has melted. It is pale in the center with gray edges. Interesting. I do it again several more times chaining the divots together into a short line. Afterwards, I let out a slow breath and a heaviness pours through me like warm liquid. I relax. Wait. I know this feeling.

Such is the way discoveries are made. For me, burning becomes the new cutting. I keep a full stash of matches hidden in my room at all times. I am determined to be smarter than I was with the cutting. Initially, I burn up high on my inner arm where even short sleeves will cover the damage. Later I decide it is safer to avoid my arms all together. Just in case.

I need a tender place that will not be seen and not raise questions. I settle on my stomach just to the right of my belly button. After that, I burn regularly for the next year or so. When one side of my stomach gets too messy, I switch to the other, then back again. I don't burn every day. In fact, sometimes I go weeks, maybe even months without burning, but when my depression returns again, heavy and suffocating, I may burn several times a day just to help me through it.

I burn when I say something stupid at school. I burn when a girl I like looks past me obliviously to flirt instead with another guy. I burn when my friends joke with me and without meaning to, they cut too close to the bone. I burn when I lose an argument with my father and have to swallow my anger. I burn because I am the ugliest guy I know.

It always makes me feel better but I'm going up in smoke.

It is my senior year now and I am sitting in my favorite class, art, which I share with Brian. We have been in art together since the sixth grade. We are sitting at our table, laughing about something, always laughing, and tuning out our teacher, Ms. Nelson.

Ms. Nelson is giving the class instructions for our next project. She scowls at Brian and me for not paying attention but continues talking. She likes us because we are both talented artists and so she cuts us a little more slack than she should. We don't return the favor. Instead we reject every attempt she makes to befriend us or teach us anything. We like art but are careful to keep ourselves separate from any stigmatizing associations it might involve. We're not about to become one of Ms. Nelson's weirdo "art fags." As if in my case it could possibly make any difference.

When she is finished with her explanation, she tells us we can begin. People begin getting to their feet and making their way to the front of the class where they will select what they will need from a supply table. As I straighten and push back my chair to join them, I feel a sudden sharp pain on my stomach that makes me suck in a breath. I look down in alarm and see a wet stain that has soaked through my shirt just to the right of my belly button. It is bloody in several spots. I realize in a sickening instant what has happened.

At this moment, the burn damage on my stomach covers a circular area roughly two inches in diameter. It is, I admit, pretty ugly but no one sees it. I don't ever bother to put a dressing on it. Why would I? Who cares? But it is getting to the point where it certainly needs one. It oozes and drains and has a scab over most of it.

While I slouched in my chair, the drainage soaked into my shirt and adhered to the fabric as it dried. When I stood up, the fabric pulled away from the wound and ripped the large scab off along with it causing the sudden sharp pain and bleeding. I stare stricken at the very conspicuous stain growing on my shirt. My private life and my public are about to collide and I am mortified.

It is like that day in the kitchen with my sister only a hundred times worse. It is not just my sister who could discover what a freak I am but my best friend. To teens, the peer group comes before all others. And so it is that Brian's opinion of me matters more than anyone else's I know. To see the look of confusion, then judgment and rejection on his face, should he find out what I have been doing, would be a crippling blow, one I doubt I could bounce back from.

I untuck my shirt from my jeans in a couple of swift moves and cover the stain with my arm as best I can while I walk. I hang a step behind Brian and hope he will not notice the stain. He doesn't, and the first chance I get, I request a bathroom break. There I retreat and wash the shirt in the sink getting the stain, at least for the most part, out. I keep my shirt untucked for the rest of the day so it doesn't stick anymore and make a promise to never burn myself again.

* * *

I don't keep the promise, but never again do I lean so

heavily on burning as a coping mechanism. Years later, into adulthood I have reached again for what I know works. It's like a former smoker who in a time of great stress thinks, "God, I'd sure love a cigarette right about now."

Depression can become so unbearable that the need for relief becomes greater than even the need to breathe. The humiliation of falling back on an adolescent coping mechanism that was even a bad idea when I actually was an adolescent and too ignorant to know any better, is over-shadowed by the simple and desperate need to just make it stop.

In time, burning, or even the desire to do so, becomes one of the many symptoms that I use to assess the severity of a depression. Familiar symptoms occur at more or less predictable intervals along an advancing depressive time-line. I often ignore the early symptoms and rationalize away their significance or role as harbingers. Later symptoms make denying the existence of depression impossible, but I still believe that I can fight it...that with the right diet and exercise plan I won't go down.

But if I am reaching again for the matches, I know I have passed a critical point in my threshold. I know I am impaired. Even if until that moment I still believed I was in control, I must admit, from that point forward, anything could happen. If there is any part of me left that still cares, and if it maintains even a toehold of control over the rest of my deteriorating mind, it tells me now is the time to see the doctor.

# Chapter 11

# A Glimpse of Things to Come

It is necessary at this point, to backtrack slightly in order to mention a particular evening I experienced in 1984. It is the first indication that perhaps there is something more than just a difficult adolescence or even depression lurking in my future. At the time, of course, I miss it completely. It wouldn't have made any difference anyway.

It is now the end of my junior year in high school, May. Some of our family from England are here visiting on a month-long vacation and staying at our house. The house is big enough for everyone but my parents decide we will be more comfortable if I give up my room and move temporarily to the playroom over the garage. This is where I am tonight.

My father designed our house himself but allowed professional builders to actually construct it. He is a do-it-yourselfer through and through, so he saved the garage for himself. When he built it, he went all out adding a couple of work and storage rooms on the side and a playroom above. The playroom has seen a lot of action through the years from us kids despite having no heating or air-conditioning. In the summer, though, on the Texas Gulf Coast no air conditioning can be a hell of a drawback and May is getting uncomfortably close to summer.

Heat and humidity aside, I am happy with the sleeping arrangements. Staying in the playroom makes me feel like I have my own apartment. I sleep on a roll away bed and keep a box fan blowing in one of the windows. The nights, like the one I am currently enjoying, are surprisingly pleasant. The thick night air feels good and the privacy is most excellent. My mood has been especially good lately. At the moment, I am laying on my bed with my hands clasped on my stomach thinking about just how wonderful everything is. Did I seriously just say that?

Maybe, I think to myself, I have at last outgrown all this sadness and self-hatred silliness. I can't even imagine feeling bad now, and the idea of killing myself? Wow. What the heck was I ever thinking? What a loser. I chuckle out loud in the dark, amused rather than embarrassed by my former self. It is a school night and I know I have to get up in the morning but I don't want to sleep. Sleep is a waste of time. Besides, I don't need that much anymore. A few hours seems plenty. I've been doing it all week. They say Einstein only slept about four hours a night. Einstein and me. Interesting. I'm just saying.

My thoughts and ideas are zipping past as I lay here and everyone is an absolute pleasure to regard. I want to consider each one of them in joyous detail, but they are like fireflies fading and winking out before I can get hold of them. I am like a child unsuccessfully trying to catch them in a jelly jar. It's maddening and yet wonderfully fun. Finally, with my empty jar, I give up and settle instead for simply watching the whole spectacle unfold.

I cannot ever remember feeling quite so happy. I am more than contented and indeed, am bordering on giddy. The breeze from this fan feels incredible on my skin. Despite the heat, I have goose bumps up my arms, neck, and scalp. Strange.

I sense the concept of time like an enormous undulating sheet of silk, how it ripples and folds, sliding against itself and straightening again, so tantalizingly close. It's right on the tip of my mind. I am certain I am on the verge of seeing beyond its illusions and understanding something funda-mental and ground-breaking about its workings. If only I could stay focused. Instead, I make a note to come back to it later. Fixating on a single idea is too confining right now. My brain is newly awake. It's stretching its legs and I'm giving it all the space it needs.

I plan my future and realize excitedly that I have the potential to accomplish the most fantastic things. I get up and pace the floor. I feel that I can do anything I set my mind to. My mouth is hanging open in a half smile and I am slowly shaking my head in amazement. I review the endless possibilities, unable to settle on any one in particu-lar because they are all so exciting, and I realize with a thrill, all within my grasp.

I could be a veterinarian. I love animals. Maybe I'd live

somewhere in England like that vet in *All Creatures Great and Small.* I could be an explorer and photographer capturing the most distant and beautiful places on the planet on film. Then I could either publish them myself in a series of coffee table type books or maybe sell them to *National Geographic.* I could attend a big Ivy League school. I'm smart enough. I've just never really tried in school. All I have to do is apply myself. I could get a scholarship, maybe study abroad at Cambridge or something. I could become an artist or a scientist. Why not? The only limits I have are the ones I set for myself.

I look out the window. God, I love the night! And tonight, for the first time in my life I love who I am. I have been so focused on my flaws that I almost missed my many talents. There are no limits for someone like me.

Wow! I can't believe how incredible I feel! Is this what if feels like to take drugs? Once again I begin to laugh and this time I can't stop. What's funny? Maybe nothing. Maybe everything. I have no idea. I laugh until tears begin to roll down my cheeks and I have to wipe them away. Gradually I regain control…mostly anyway. I can feel the laugh still inside me, though, pressure loaded, ready to explode again at the slightest provocation…or maybe at no provocation at all. Whatever. Who cares.

Now I stop my pacing and just stand in the middle of the floor. My arms slowly float out from my sides as if they are weightless as my thoughts continue to accelerate. Goose bumps once again break out across my skin again and I feel them all the way to my ankles. The sensation is amazing.

I want to just stand there and enjoy it, but wait! No! Shit! I have to go outside right now. Why didn't I think of it sooner? I rush outside to the large balcony and look around in every direction. Oh man! The night is beautiful. I look up at the stars and am astounded by how many I can see. The leaves on the tree growing up next to the balcony rustle in the gentle night breeze but I hear them as if they are mere inches from my head whispering secrets and promises into my ears. My brain is processing everything with laser-like precision. I feel so buoyant that I think I may be lifted right off the balcony and carried away on the wind.

It is, by this point, after 2:00 in the morning. Everyone is asleep. Are you kidding me? No one is seeing this gorgeous night sky except me? I snort. Their loss.

It occurs to me in a sort of epiphany that everything in the universe is interconnected like the gears and wheels of an expensive watch, each part, no matter how small, necessary and integral in the precision of the whole. Each and every part perfect. I am part of this perfection. I am not just seeing the stars, I am part of them and them of me! Am I having some kind of religious experience? Is God trying to communicate with me? I can't stop smiling!

You know what would feel great right now? Running. Speed. Hell, yes! I want to feel the wind on my face. It's the perfect thing. I can't waste this night. I have to run now and experience speed with this new hunger for life I'm feeling! I'm alive and I want more!

The balcony was a last afterthought in the construction of our garage and, at the time, my father just sort of ran out of steam and lost interest in the project. As such, a number of the final details were never added…like a railing for the deck. This convenient oversight, I am certain, could have occurred for no other reason than to make it unnecessary for me to now climb over. So with nothing to stand in my way, I run right off the second floor balcony and launch myself into the night. Into the future. Who has time for stairs? Not me.

When I hit, I tuck and roll, then bounce up and shoot off across the yard. I sprint from one side to the other circling and wheeling like one of those crazed little Frisbee dogs that go tearing around just for the fun of it. It feels like flying. I don't want to stop. So I don't. I keep at it till I am breathless and exhausted. At last when I've had my fill of speed, I climb the stairs back up to my lair. I am tired but still deliriously happy and I have no idea why.

I don't go to sleep even then. I want to enjoy the night a while longer. I plan some more and promise myself to remember all my insights. This is the new me, the real me. Never again will I be my old gloomy self. I have a new perspective. If I ever want to die again, I tell myself, I will leave my life behind, go and live with Tibetan monks or something. It's desperate, sure, but not as desperate as suicide. An escape is really all a person needs, not death. Life is precious and wonderful. As I finally drift into a contented sleep, I am confident that when my alarm goes off in another hour or two I will still feel the same.

The high has peaked though. There are echoes of it when I wake and through the next day, but the intensity has faded. I remain in a good mood for the next couple of days but that is all. The pure joy and exhilaration do not return. The good mood and fast thinking do not escalate and never spin out of control. Instead the magic of that night just sifts through my fingers like sand and there is nothing I can do to prevent it.

My dreams of studying at Cambridge on scholarship or being a country veterinarian that makes house calls disappear along with my optimism for life. When it is gone I am left alone, as I will be over and over again in my life, wondering in confusion, what the hell was I thinking? I never tell anyone about the incident. It is private and I doubt anyone would understand it anyway. I don't understand it myself... not yet.

* * *

Years later, I learn that when adolescents first begin to experience symptoms of bipolar disorder their mood swings are shorter in duration than those of adults. Highs and lows might last hours or days and in time they lengthen to weeks or months. What I experienced that night in the playroom in 1984 was probably my first taste of euphoria. Euphoria is defined as intense feelings of happiness and energy. It is something I will experience numerous times but to differing degrees. For me it comes, if it's going to come at all, in the early stages of a manic episode. It could last anywhere from a couple of hours to a couple of days, but like a cool breeze on a summer afternoon, it is always gone too soon.

In my case, euphoria has always proven elusive and impossible to predict. It is not a part of every manic episode or even necessarily the most intense. It is a rare and special event that surprises me each time it visits. It is always welcome and I ride it happily until it passes. Bipolar disorder can take away so much. In my experience, euphoria is one of the few things it grudgingly gives back in return.

# Chapter 12

# The New Me

In the fall of 1985 I begin attending Stephen F. Austin State University. Noted for its beautiful campus and beautiful girls, SFA is the soul of Nacogdoches, a sleepy college town situated in the heart of the East Texas piney woods. The moment I turn onto campus from North Street, I know I have found my new home.

A college campus is a special place, a different world. This is a world where sidewalks wind lazily through a maze of mismatched dorms and academic buildings. Where Frisbees are thrown on thick sun-dappled lawns beneath towering live oaks and pines. It is a world that slows but never completely sleeps

Here in this world everyone I pass is my age. Everyone is excited about their future. They all have a plan. They walk with backpacks slung over a shoulder or glide by on ten speeds, always on their way to somewhere. Here the landscaping is flawless, azaleas and crape myrtles forever blooming in pinks and whites. Outdoor bulletin boards are covered with homemade flyers announcing parties, events, and unknown bands playing the local clubs. Here, each autumn, during Saturday afternoon football games, the excitement is electric and the distant roar of the stadium crowd drifts on the air like fallen leaves.

I am accompanied to SFA by and share a dorm room with another close friend from high school, Jake. Jake started to hang out with Brian and me around our sophomore year when we all ran track together. He is a tall good looking kid, a former nerd, not quite reformed. He has a quirky sense of humor, drinks way too much, and possesses a fearlessness that breeds in him an easy willingness to go first in whatever harebrained schemes we or our friends have come up with. He has terrible judgment and no inhibitions at all. If he doesn't get you thrown out of them, he is hilarious at parties, and he can fix absolutely anything. We get along impossibly well and will, for the next four years, have one hell of a good time.

My first semester at SFA, though, I am still so emotionally disabled that I should have a parking placard. By the age of 19 I have, it's true, left many of my more homely features behind me. Teeth have been straightened, braces removed, glasses replaced by contacts, limbs grown into… more or less. It is an improvement for me to be sure, but the preceding years I spent viewing myself with such pitiless cruelty have twisted my self-image to the extent that I can see no difference in myself from then to now. To my eyes, I remain a gangly big nosed, acne covered troll, so sickening that I could turn the world's collective stomach. This is not a helpful attitude to have when trying to meet girls, and yet, my failings do not end there.

Because I was such an introvert in high school, I came to college with only the most rudimentary social skills. It would be laughable if it wasn't so painful trying to develop them here. I am a horrible wall flower at parties, have yet to step on a dance floor, am clueless in bars; have no idea how to talk to girls, or anyone other than Jake for that matter, and do I even need to say it? I am a virgin.

Considering that everyone else here is already competent at so many things that I am petrified to even try, I feel my inadequacy all the more. My faults do not go unnoticed by those around me either and my self-esteem takes another battering in the first year here. Still, I enjoy myself more than I did in high school and manage at least a sort of a blooming.

Depression still dogs me. No surprise. It is as much a part of me as the color of my eyes or my ruined self-esteem. Jake is aware that I am struggling and tries his best to help me when he can but there is only so much he can do. He knows, in a general way, that I am sensitive and get depressed. He knows I am a little too intense and overreact to situations, but he has no idea how black and how dangerous my despair goes.

Living in close quarters with so many guys my own age has both advantages and disadvantages. The obvious advantage is that it is fun. A dorm is a place of non-stop activity. Practical jokes, laughter, support, and companionship are so ever present that it is easy to take them for granted. It is an experience not to be missed. The disadvantage, though, if you view it that way, is the lack of privacy. You are rarely ever alone. For me, however, this turns out to be a good thing as well.

In high school I separated my dark side from my socially acceptable side. I kept the dark side confined, at least as much as I could confine it, to when I was alone. In a college dorm there is no place for that. No time to feel maudlin or hopeless. No time to mope or read poetry. There is no place for me to privately burn myself or lay around thinking about death, longing for nothingness like it were a beach in Cancun. And in truth, this is exactly what I need. I hate the person I was in high school. I hate his weakness and am determined to be better than that. I will not have a private side of me that is shameful. I will be normal, at all times, nothing to hide.

Wanting to be someone new and actually being someone new are, for me, two conditions not easily united. Crossing the gulf that exists between them will take some work. I am already somewhat of an expert at faking it, of hiding my wretchedness from other people. I honed that skill in high school. I decide, in a flash of inspiration that if this is going to work, what I need to do now is somehow hide it from myself. Now that would be true genius!

The analogy I use to reason out the whole thing out goes like this. Life is a superhighway and we are all speeding along it. Our driving experience is unavoidably dependent on the car we are given to make the journey in. This kind of stinks as my own car is a hoopty of the worst sort. It is an offense to regular automobiles and has no business being on the road at all.

As such, I have kept my little beater to the access road without much complaint. I am puttering along at 30 mph or so and watching the rest of the world race by me. One by one, everyone I know leaves me vanishing in their rear-view mirrors. They go flying down the highway with the cruise control set at 75 in the fast lane like it was the most natural thing in the world. They relax in their late model SUVs with the windows up, the A/C blowing, a CD in the stereo, and a Coke in the cup holder. They don't even notice me over here on the access road, and thank God for that. But this is not the life I want.

I want to be up there in the flow. I hate myself and this ridiculous jalopy so I decide to say, "Fuck it!" At the next chance I will swerve over and mash the accelerator to the floor. I will roar up the on ramp and into traffic. I know my car can't handle the strain. It's never going to make the whole trip if I do this but I don't care. Making the whole trip is not my objective. Something terrible is not only going to happen but it is going to happen sooner more likely than later. The engine will seize or the whole thing will catch fire before I get too far but that's still the best play by far. Better to go up in a fireball halfway along than to make it the whole distance staying on the access road.

I'll pull up alongside of the other drivers and wave to them smiling. They'll think I'm one of them. They'll have no idea that my tachometer is red-lining or that I have no A/C and am sweating my ass off. They'll never see the smoke coming in through my vents or feel the ominous shuddering coming from under my seat.

And as for me, I'll fool myself as well. I won't look at the tachometer. I'll ignore the smoke. I'll block out the shuddering. And I'll turn up the radio so I can't hear the screaming protests of the engine.

I will have no regrets when the day comes and everything falls apart, but why worry about that today? It might be a week off or decade from now. Who knows? Who cares? Worrying is for chumps. Punch it!

So this is my plan. I pretend I am normal and by golly, I sell it. I hide my true self away again and this time I bury it so deep that even I do not remember who I was before. And if I do say so myself, it works. At least it works in a half-ass sort of way. I laugh, I study, I make friends. I manage to date a few girls and to my surprise they are even pretty, though I always ruin the relationships given a little time. Somewhere along the way I even lose my virginity. Boo ya. I go to parties. I learn to dance or do something that passes for it. And I make the dean's list every semester.

As an incoming freshman I selected art as my major but art is an ill fit for my new phony self. When other kids said they were majoring in business or finance or engineering, I felt embarrassed by my own choice. Even now I don't want to be taken for one of Ms. Nelson's skinny pot smoking ilk.

My sophomore year, I change my major to nutrition and distance myself a little farther from who I used to be. It is the first of many majors I'll try out before it's all said and done. I get rid of all my art supplies and bury my talent along with the rest of my past. It will be more than a decade before I uncover it again.

My transformation to normalcy is not as impressive as it seems on the surface. I am, after all, a dangerous smoking rattletrap of a young man who's pushing himself beyond his limits trying to keep up with the world, ignoring all the blinking warning lights on his dashboard. I could fly into pieces at any moment. If anyone looks closely enough at me they will see the strain on my face, maybe a tremor in my hands. Jake sees what it's all costing me because we live together, but he is too good a friend to mention it.

# Chapter 13

# Can't Slow Down

The marginal success I enjoy at college is accomplished with the help of a new and more socially acceptable coping mechanism—exercising. Like the cutting and burning of old, exercising provides a desperately needed conduit to release the black feelings that build up inside me. As an added bonus, exercising is a respected, even admirable, activity. Good cover.

Exercising also gives me a modicum of control over my physical appearance. It gives me something I can change about myself that I hope will offset the numerous things that I can't. Where most aspects of who I am feel chiseled-in-stone-permanent, my body is different. I can change my body. I can make it better. All I have to do is work hard. It's not much, but it's something and when you hate everything about yourself down to the smallest detail, a little hope is all you need to get yourself through the day.

So I lift weights, a lot. I work out every day. I go to

aerobics classes. I run, miles and miles around the campus and at the stadium. I bicycle, and I play. I play Frisbee, volleyball, tennis, anything I can tire myself out doing. I stay in constant motion. I have always been an athlete, not great at any particular sport but coordinated and able to pick up most anything in a short time and then do it passably well.

It helps. It does not give me the proverbial runner's high but rather creates a stabilizing counterforce to push back against the force of a mind turned against itself. It props up my self-esteem enough to allow me to function. Unfortunately it is just about the only thing that does. This façade of mental stability is completely one dimensional. I know it is too, but one dimension is still better than no dimensions at all. My ability to look people in the eyes instead of staring at the floor, or to be able to smile or laugh is all precariously dependent on nothing more than what I believe to be my current level of fitness.

Because of this, I work out beyond what is healthy. It becomes an addiction. I regularly overtrain. I suffer from one exercise-related injury after another because I push my body past where it should be pushed. I become depressed each time I miss a workout. As usual, I take it too far.

Whenever I am upset or the bully, aka my Censor, is ranting too loudly for me to stand it, you can find me in the weight room lifting...past failure, past burnout, straining both muscles and joints alike. If not there, I will be cycling somewhere, my legs pumping like pistons or maybe at the stadium running myself mindlessly to exhaustion, forever trying to undo things that cannot be undone and control things that cannot be controlled. I achieve in this, I suppose, a level of unhealthy fitness. It's the best I can do.

# Chapter 14

# Death Wish

While exercising helps me to cope with my frustrations, self-hate, and overall gloomy disposition, it has its limits. My depressions still seem able to drive right over my defenses at least a time or two each semester. When they do, thoughts of death are inevitably riding shotgun. For all my changes, I am discouraged to see that, in regards to living, the urge to *give* up is at least as powerful as the urge to *keep* up, and it returns to me over and over again. It makes me feel weak, like maybe I belong on the access road after all, but there's no way I'm going back.

I try to push down my suicidal thoughts, deny them like everything else, but these urges are no light weights. If not addressed and dealt with properly, they will find a way to come out, one way or another. They will not stay buried for long.

While I am able to, at least ostensibly, remove the option of suicide from my game plan, it turns out that killing myself by indirect means is still very much in play. So now

I become a danger seeker, a risk taker, and a fate tempter. I participate in any activity that is self-destructive and has a chance of getting me killed. In many ways this becomes my identity for years to come. Friends think I am wild and exciting, in a crazy sort of way. I am more than willing to risk my life at the drop of a hat for a rush. If I live, I have a great story to tell and if I die, well, even better.

As friends and roommates, Jake and I do most things together. This includes taking unnecessary risks. Though for Jake it is different I think. He does the things we do for the simple thrill of them. He is full of the hubris of youth, believing he is invincible and nothing bad can ever happen to him. With this sense of naive bravado he not only keeps up but often surpasses me in acts of sheer stupidity. Still, it is difficult to compete with me over the long haul. I can almost always go farther, cut it closer, or push it farther simply because I am the one secretly harboring a death wish. It's hardly fair.

We ride motorcycles…way too fast, we binge drink, we climb up the outsides of buildings, we elevator surf. Elevator surfing is the asinine act of climbing onto the roof of an elevator car and riding it up and down the elevator shaft. Jake and I would usually take this a step farther and climb around the shaft itself as well, sometimes more than ten stories up. I would hang from the cables like a monkey and jump from car to car dodging the stack of speeding counter weights that move in opposition to the elevator cars, often in near total darkness.

In the summer break of 1986 during a torrential

downpour and subsequent flood, I jump with a co-worker into a rain swollen creek just for fun. The creek has over-flowed its banks and is doing a pretty good imitation of some class V rapids. We are immediately swept away in its powerful current and laugh about it, joking that we can now swim like Johnny Weissmuller. Some distance downstream we encounter a jam of logs, branches, and debris and are slammed against them by the irresistible force of the water at our back. No longer moving with it, we suddenly experi-ence the full power of the flood.

Choking as the brown water cascades over our heads and pushes our legs deeper into the tangle below, we quickly determine that there is no choice but to go down or drown. Taking a lungful of air we each submerge, make our way to the bottom where we pick our way methodically through the jam. On the other side we pop up as carefree as a couple of Labradors gasping and laughing and continue downstream. Another story to tell.

One moonless night Jake and I swim out into an enor-mous man-made pond and climb down into a cement tower there. The tower is part of a system designed to keep the water level of the pond consistent. As the water in the pond rises due to inflow from the creeks that feed it, the excess cascades down into the tower through a square window cut in the side. At the bottom, some 10 to 15 feet below the surface, it is washed into a culvert. The culvert, in turn, carries it beneath the pond and through the base of a levy then shoots out into another run-off creek on the other side. So on this particular night, hunching at the bottom of the tower being pummeled by a torrent of falling water, and in impenetrable blackness, we decide to go along for the ride. If that isn't enough, we do it with no clear idea of what will happen to us or what is down there. Could we be bigger idiots? Sadly, the answer is yes.

We jump across railroad tracks in front of speeding trains at the last conceivable second nearly giving the engineers a coronary as they blast their horns at us. I keep at this for months always trying to break my own record until I cut it so insanely close that afterwards I have to sit alone on a post for several long minutes to recover my composure. During that time I am literally unable to speak. It is the last time I track jump. There is no longer any point to it. I know that I have set a record that cannot be broken.

Jake and I also climb a 1,500 foot broadcast tower at night during a thunderstorm and watch as the lightning actually flashes below us. On this bit of hijinks we are accompanied by a third and also slightly off-kilter friend named Jeff. At the top we all take pictures of each other hanging out over the edge. It occurs to us far too late that for each minute we spent on top we were being microwaved within an inch of our lives.

We climb back down in a rush, certain that we are all now sterile. In my case, it would surely be for the best.

I think nothing of climbing out of the passenger window of a speeding pick-up truck into the rear bed for no better reason than to ride back there a while. On more than one occasion I jump back and forth between two convertibles while racing down the highway. We tow a hang glider behind my MG Midget taking turns flying while the other one drives. The ways to kill oneself are endless and I'm having the time of my life trying them all...daring any of them to take me.

## Chapter 15

# What Am I Doing?

I return home for the summer of 1987. It is the only summer I will do so. Gulfview is only about twenty minutes from Galveston Island and the Gulf of Mexico. It was one of the few benefits of growing up here. When we are home, my friends and I still like to take advantage of it.

One night after work Jake and I drive down to Galveston, park, and walk onto the free ferry that carries cars back and forth between Galveston and the Bolivar Peninsula. We go just for the ride, something to do. The ferry pulls away and begins its slow chug across the bay. We stand at the rail and look out into the night talking and feeling the sway of the ocean beneath us. About midway across with the lights of Galveston and Bolivar twinkling on twin horizons, I am struck with an idea of such brilliance that I can scarcely contain myself.

I beg Jake to jump overboard with me. Right then in all our clothes. See if we can make the swim. It is so dark no one would see us, I explain. No one would alert the captain. No one would stop the ferry. No one would throw us a life ring. We could just disappear into the darkness in the ferry's wake. We are walk-on traffic so we have no car to worry about. It's perfect! And if you are thinking, well, that's just crazy though, isn't it? Good, then you're beginning to get the idea.

Jake must think so too and speaking from the unaccustomed role of the voice of reason, he vetoes the idea. I consider going it alone for several tense minutes. My adrenaline is already surging and like a child, I have always had difficulty changing gears once I have made a plan. In the end Jake manages to keep me on the ferry and I reluctantly let the idea go.

Another incident later that same summer opens my eyes to the folly of this type of self-delusion. I convince Jake, Brian, and our friend Jeff from the infamous broadcast tower climb, that we should climb a newly constructed water tower in town that has not yet been filled with water and have a little fun. We reach the top from the inside, clamber out of a hatch and walk around on the summit looking down at the lights of the city.

I turn to Jeff, whom I have known since high school. "You ready?" I ask him grinning.

"Ready," he confirms with an equally idiotic grin.

The original idea I sold them is that when we reached the top, I would crab walk down the curving surface of the tank and spray paint a mark when I could go no farther. Later, we would try to see if the mark was visible from the ground.

Jeff, however, has elected to go with me and spray a mark of his own. We decide to make it a contest and see who had the nerve to lower themselves the farthest without sliding off the side of the tower and plunging to their death. Sound planning.

Jake holds the two cans of spray paint we have brought with us while Jeff and I remove our shoes and socks and set them aside. For this, we are going to need bare feet. Oh, and we're going to need to be lunatics. Check!

I stand, take a can from Jake, and wedge it into my pocket. This way I'll be able to keep both of my hands free until I'm ready to paint. Jeff does the same and we give each other a nod. It's time.

We walk away from our friends and quickly disappear below the horizon of the tank disappearing like a couple of Columbus's ships. When I can go no farther I lower myself to my seat and place my hands next to me. The surface of the metal tank is cool. It's still dry but beginning to edge toward clammy. It's perfect for a friction descent so I lift my hips and continue down.

In this way, I am able to crab down maybe another six feet or so. When my heart is banging in my chest and my entire blood supply has been replaced by adrenaline, I stop at last. I am scared shitless. I am so far down the curving surface that my weight threatens to pull me off the side at any second. I feel if I move a muscle, I will shoot off into nothingness and the next thing I feel I feel will be the hard earth 110 feet below.

I look over at Jeff a short distance to my left. He too is

frozen at about the same point. Gone are our grins. Moving slowly with the care of bomb diffusers we shift our weight enough to free one hand and remove the spray cans from our pockets. We each make our marks and then drop the cans. Getting them back into our pockets is not worth the risk. I just want to get two hands back on the tank. I wish a helicopter would come and pluck us off the side. We're too far down and I know it. While we are able to hold our position, I fear that the initial push it will require to start moving back up toward the top will be too much. One or both of us has a very high likelihood of falling. Still, we can't sit here all night, so we roll the dice yet again and begin the slow crabbing climb back up the side.

At last and to our relief, we reach the relative safety of the summit and our waiting friends. Our friends had not seen or heard from us in several long minutes, and didn't know if both or either of us would return this time. It was a reasonable concern.

The following day under the afternoon sun we drive by the water tank to look up at it by the light of day. There, to my quiet horror, are both spray painted marks impossibly far down on the sides of the tank. For us to have been that far down without any safety ropes and somehow made it back up again was beyond miraculous. The realization of what we had done raises the hair on the back of my neck. God protects fools and drunks.

It is at this moment I see the flaw in my behavior. I see with sickening clarity the irresponsibility that I have shown toward my friends who are truly dear to me. I see how easily

I could have killed or disabled any one of them with these stunts. I love them all like brothers. I know their parents and families. How could I not have thought of them? I was so busy carelessly disregarding my own safety that I never considered the safety of those around me. I feel hot shame for my sins and gratitude to God for not making my friends pay the price for them.

After the water tower incident I am more careful. I still seek out recklessly self-destructive activities but try to do the most life-threatening things alone. I even abandon a few of my own ideas when I consider the unacceptable risk to my friends' lives. More and more I just keep my ideas to myself. I imagine stepping out into traffic, or dropping out of the car door onto the freeway at high speed. At times I actually beg God to take me and it gets worse when my depressions are severe or accompanied by agitation.

To my very great shame it is usually Jake who I continue to drag along to join me while I play Russian Roulette with my life. He is always willing and his arrogant certainty that nothing bad will ever happen to him makes me believe it as well. Thankfully we are both right.

# Chapter 16

# Hurricane Jerry

On October 16, 1989, Hurricane Jerry makes landfall on Galveston Island packing sustained winds of 85 mph with gusts over a 100. I am there. As you might expect. Wouldn't miss this.

Jake and I have driven down from Nacogdoches for the occasion and take an inflatable Zodiac-type boat with a 10 horsepower motor on it out into Galveston Bay during the height of the storm. We manage, somewhat miraculously, to get it maybe half a mile to a mile out, (it's hard for me to judge distance on the water) powering up and over the steepest and most frightening breakers I have ever been in before.

As we climb each new wave, we fall on top of each other at the transom of the boat, the bow pointing straight into the slate gray sky as the engine strains wide open to make it to the top. Sometimes our timing is good but more often than not the wave curls over and comes crashing down on our heads with the indifferent weight of the whole ocean.

When we crest the wave the boat teeter totters at the top. The prop comes free from the water, RPMs screaming, and we go careening down into the trough on the other side. In the process we nearly tumble out over the bow, again, one on top of the other. At last we clear the breakers and motor out into the only slightly less violent swells.

We are shouting at each other, in part from fear and adrenaline and in part to be heard over the cacophony of the storm. It sounds like we're boating right into the exhaust port of a 747 jet engine. When our own small engine sputters and stalls a short while later, we can hardly hear the difference. We both know the significance of it though.

Being adrift without power in these seas is serious trouble. Jake begins to yank on the starting chord but the motor folds its arms across its chest and ignores him.

"Can you get it started?" I ask stupidly.

"Trying," he says without losing focus. He reprimes it and tries again. The motor coughs but has no intention of catching. It has made up its mind.

"We may have gotten water in it," Jake calls over his shoulder. Yeah, maybe. He continues to yank on the starter but the motor is having none of it. So much sea water has broken over us it would be a miracle if the engine isn't full of it. The boat sure is.

Water sloshes back and forth right up to the gunwales. Thankfully the boat is inflatable so it doesn't affect our buoyancy. A small cooler is floating on its side, the lid is gone. Several unopened beers, those that did not join the lid in the ocean, are bobbing around like ducks in a bathtub.

I consider our situation…of course it's dire. It all feels embarrassingly familiar. Every now and again another beer drifts out over the side with a swell and disappears into the bay like a message in a bottle. The fact that we brought beer with us at all only goes to prove what senseless imbeciles we are.

The boat is rising and falling on swells that look like office buildings and we cannot even see land. Rain is slashing across us almost horizontally stinging our skin like bees. We can see it coming in heavy bands across the water. And still the engine will not start.

Jake lifts the cowling and makes some adjustments to the motor inside. After a moment he replaces it and tries again. Nothing. "I think we're fucked," he shouts over the wind.

I look around us in all directions at the gray and raging storm. While we focused our attention on the engine, the boat had been drifting and turning. Now everything looks the same. The power is out all over the island so there are no lights in the distance to use as a reference. I am, for the moment, confused. Our exact position and orientation is unknown.

The boat continues to soar as it is lifted on each swell, then drops nauseatingly into next trough. We have no oars. Why would we? Preparation is for amateurs. Chumps. And besides, which direction would we paddle if we did? Visibility is for shit. It's like another world out here. I look back at Jake and smile sheepishly.

"It's possible," I say. "That this may not have been the best idea."

Jake smiles back. "Ya think?" He looks around squinting into the rain, then shouts over the din, "What do you think we should do?"

"I dunno," I yell back and mean it. We needn't worry though. The decision of what to do next is about to be made for us.

Something changes, something indefinable and unsettling. That strange sense of urgency that makes a gazelle look up from the watering hole sounds an alarm in my head and I stiffen. Then I feel it, the approach of something dark and ominous from behind me. The boat accelerates sliding sideways in the grip of something massive. I snap my head around and see a towering black wall of water materialize off our starboard side. It is a mountain of a wave and it's closing fast on us out of the gray nebula storm.

"Paddle!" we both shout in unison. I plunge my arm into the water alongside the boat and pull for all I am worth. Seeing Jake do the same on the other side of the boat, I switch to back paddling on my side in order to turn the boat. We are desperately trying to swing the unwieldy bow around to meet our attacker head on but there is no time. The wave is upon us. It overtakes us and we shoot up the face of it broadside. We both see the inevitable capsize coming and know there is no way to stop it.

Helplessly, I watch as the sea and the sky roll over and change places. Then I am weightless. It is almost peaceful but it doesn't last. An instant later I am pounded into the sea as if by the fist of a giant.

I know better than to fight the force of water. Plenty

of near drownings have taught me that so I stay relaxed. I am tumbled and jerked one way then another but am not alarmed. I have a lung full of air and can hold my breath like a porpoise so I am in no hurry. Only when the wave has passed and its churning currents have released me do I venture back the way my middle ear assures me is up. My head breaks the surface and I re-enter the violent world of the storm.

Between the driving rain and the whipping spindrift, the difference between air and ocean is negligible at best, but I can at least breathe. I turn in a circle treading water and look for Jake. At first I don't see him but then as I am lifted high by another immense swell I spot him, his head like a dark coconut on the water about 15 yards from me.

The boat is gone. How did we get separated so far from each other that fast, I wonder. The currents here must be crazy strong. The distance between us is already widening. I hear him shout something at me but it's lost on the wind. I give him a thumbs up to let him know I'm okay and he brings his arm over his head in a high arc then makes a chopping motion to his left indicating which way we should swim. An instant later he disappears into a trough and I do not see him again till we are both on the beach.

It is clear to me by this point what happened. All the while we were drifting and bobbing on the swells trying to sort out the engine, those 85 mph winds were pushing us back toward Galveston. Before we had realized it, we had reached the outermost breakers again where we were tossed like a toy by the first wave in a set. That meant that there was good news and bad news.

Normally breakers mean land, but that is not always the case. Here, the sea floor makes a long and gradual approach toward the beach at Galveston and it is striped with countless sandbars. As a consequence, the breakers here form at intervals, some of which are, in fact, absurdly far from shore. On the way out it seemed that each time we cleared one set of breakers there was simply another one out in front of us in the distance. The bad news is that I am being manhandled, err, ocean handled, by what surely are the most distant of those breakers. It means I still have one hell of a swim ahead of me. The good news though is that now at least I know which way to swim. The ocean is pointing the way home.

I do not worry about Jake. He is both stronger and faster than me and almost as good in the water. I know he can take care of himself. In truth I am more at ease than I have been since we put to sea. Oriented again, and no longer with a boat or roommate that I have any way to help, my responsibility shrinks to myself alone.

I do not fear drowning. Much. I have always been at home in the water and am confident in my ability here. So I relax and set myself to the task. In honesty I am enjoying myself tremendously. The whole thing seems surreal, being alone in the roughest seas I have ever been in without so much as a life jacket. And not a soul here apart from Jake who is also out here surviving. It almost makes me laugh.

I swim through the first set of breakers, across an endless expanse of swells, then into the next set of breakers. I do this several times until at last I can see the beach, indistinct through the gloom. It is not all I see. Up ahead of me to my surprise I spot our capsized Zodiac face down battered and drifting toward the same beach. I swim faster wondering if I can catch up with it.

As I close in, I am lifted from behind by an enormous wave. The timing is perfect so I use it to my advantage. I windmill my tired arms furiously to accelerate with the wave. When I feel it has me tight in its grip and will not leave me behind I stiffen my body, lock my arms to my sides and arch my back. The wave and I are now one, roaring toward the Zodiac with me sticking out of the front of it like the prow on a pirate ship.

The gap between myself and the boat is being eaten up fast. I can now see the boat, which is going in toward the beach stern first, is trailing its painter line out behind it. I am moving well and wonder if I will be able to reach it in time.

A human body is only so hydrodynamic though. I cannot stay with the wave all the way in like a surfboard, so after a good ride I slide through the top of the wave and into the trailing trough just as I was about to reach the end of the painter. I know the Zodiac is only about a second from being lifted and taken away by the same wave that has just delivered me here and so my opportunity will be lost.

With this in mind, I make a desperate lunge for the trailing painter. I just close my fingers around it when my arm is half yanked from its socket as the wave claims its next prize. It works and I am off again being pulled like a skier behind the fleeing Zodiac.

This happens a couple of more times before I can reel myself in and secure a better grip on the grab line that encircles the boat. I have been swimming for what feels like forever now and am too beat to bother trying to heave myself up on top of the upturned deck. Instead I just rest and dangle there letting the surf do all the remaining work.

When at last my feet touch the sandy bottom I walk with the boat the rest of the way in, stumbling here and there as waves crash against my back. The beach is almost gone but I drag the boat up onto a tiny strip of sand that has yet to be covered by the storm surge. I am nearly in the parking lot. Which parking lot? I have no idea.

I sit on the boat and look down to what's left of the beach into the howling gale. There walking toward me looking cold and well-drenched, but otherwise none the worse for wear, is my roommate. He is grinning stupidly and, I suspect, has just enjoyed himself as much as I have.

Once he arrives and we give each other a brief account of our swim to shore we agree on the probable location of his car. Out of the water now, we are both shivering so we don't waste time. We flip the boat over and start back dragging it in the shallows behind us.

About halfway to the car we encounter two guys maybe in their late twenties walking up the beach toward us.

"Did you guys take that out there?" one of them asks nodding at our boat.

"Yeah," Jake answers. "Didn't end well though. The engine stalled and we were capsized. Had to swim in."

I feel a little ridiculous. It sounds even stupider when

you just say it right out. We wait for the usual response, "you guys are fucking crazy," but it doesn't come.

"Whoa," says one sounding impressed.

"Yeah, it's pretty rough out there," says the other. Then, "We just wrecked our sailboat on the jetty back there." He thumbs back over his shoulder somewhere and the two of them laugh.

Jake raises his eyebrows. I blink. "You guys took a sailboat out in this?" I say.

"Yup," says the first guy.

"So messed up, man," says the second with a surfer laugh. Then they turn and continue up the beach laughing at themselves as they go.

Jake and I walk along in silence for a few minutes. "Those guys are crazier than we are," I say.

Jake considers this a moment then mumbles, "Doubtful," and we trudge on through the stinging rain.

Several days after returning to Stephen F. Austin, I think back on my latest adventure and recognize a surprising difference between it and the countless adventures that came before it. Introspection, at this age, is something I avoid. I am more interested in hiding things from myself than discovering them. From time to time, however, I do have to take stock of things in order to make adjustments to my plans as needed. This is one of those times because if what I think has occurred, has in fact occurred, it will change everything.

Was boating into the teeth of a hurricane both exciting and fun? The prosecutor me asks the defendant me.

Definitely. Was doing so both moronic and dangerous as hell? Without a doubt. Did you do it, however, with any dark ulterior motive in mind that did not involve fun? No. Was it self-destructive in any way? I shake my head in wonder. Absolutely not. The jury gasps.

In fact, Mister, errr…me…when was the last time you made *any* serious attempt to flirt with death? I can't even remember. Okay, then this brings me to the million-dollar question. Do you still want, secretly or otherwise, to die? And here's the thing, no. I don't. Well, I'll be damned.

I don't know at what point the false me supplanted the real me but that is what happened. I am him…or he is me… whatever. The point is, maybe I will make it after all. Maybe all the humiliating melancholia I lived with for so long is truly part of my past. It belongs to the weakling I was in high school but perhaps…I am no more.

I'm living now just like everyone else. I attend my classes. I pay my bills. I laugh. I shake hands. I flirt with girls, if a little clumsily. I have friends. I even have a future for God's sake. And although it's difficult at times I see for the first time, I am up to the challenge. Maybe I belong up here on the freeway after all. Who'd have thought it?

After this, my self-destructive behavior comes, for the most part, to an end. It is long overdue. I am far from the poster boy for mental health, but from now on, my enjoyment begins to come from activities that are neither hazardous nor life-threatening. They're just fun. What a concept.

## Chapter 17

## Mostly Normal

I finish college with a degree in nursing. It is an unlikely choice for my career path and not all that well-thought out but it secures me a job right after graduation and that is important to me. Too many of my friends were back living at home with their parents and looking for work even years after earning their degrees. I wanted no part of that.

My first job brings me to Dallas, where after a short break-in period, I begin to grow into my new role as a nurse. I work on a busy surgical floor but float to trauma when the staffing there is thin. To my surprise I find that although the work is stressful I am suited to it. I enjoy having the opportunity to ease other people's suffering when I can. It is a perk that not many jobs offer so directly. I am by this time married to my first wife and enter into the quiet years of my life.

By quiet years I do not necessarily mean happy years although they certainly are at times. My wife and I are both immature and too damaged in one way or another to build a successful or lasting marriage together but we're too young to realize it, so we venture out into life at each other's sides and don't make a complete mess of it, not yet.

Life is forgiving and our responsibilities few so we enjoy ourselves traveling and socializing as a couple while figuring out how to be grown-ups along the way. Except for a few hiccups, my mind seems to be on solid ground for the first time in years and my depression is apparently on a welcome hiatus. I assume, as always, that it must obviously be gone. If I mention my gloomy past at all, I do so only in the vaguest of terms saying that I may have had a little more difficulty surviving adolescence than most kids.

One of the hiccups I do experience however is rage. Perhaps rage is too strong a word but I don't know how else to refer to it. It does not happen often but when it does it seems uncontrollable. I do not angrily flip the bird to drivers who cut me off. I do not get in fist fights or knock my wife around. I have not hit another person in anger since high school. It is inanimate objects rather that I vent my anger upon.

Dishes, furniture, cabinet doors, lawn equipment, etc. None of these are safe if my explosive temper is tapped. I never know what will set me off in a fury, but when something does, checking my behavior is like trying to keep my eyes open while sneezing. When it ignites, I want to smash everything within reach.

Since triggers are usually too small to account for the anger that erupts from me, I assume I must have a well of anger in me hiding just below the surface ready to explode without a moment's notice. I am confused by this anger and afraid of it. I know it is not normal.

When I have one of these outbursts, my wife assures me that it is frightening to see. I can think of few things as degrading as being told by my wife that my temper has scared her. I am normally so laid back. How could I do something so out of character…something so "domestic violencey"?

I struggle to understand why it is that I sometimes lose control this way. I suppose it could be that I am immature and, in my early twenties, have too much circulating testosterone. Maybe sometimes it just gets the better of me like "roid" rage, the hair trigger temper experienced by people using steroids. Deep down though I am certain that more than anything else it is because I am a bad person. It is one more character flaw I have to be ashamed of.

It never occurs to me that this type of anger could be a symptom of a gathering illness. It never occurs to me that there may be two sides of me like two great tectonic plates, and that, although still years away from a real quake, they are beginning to chafe against each another and set off tell-tale sparks.

I avoid personal conflicts as a precaution to avoid an outburst. I try to get along with everyone, sometimes to a fault. I cannot afford, though, to have the wrong button pushed. I do not trust myself or my unpredictable anger. Experience has taught me that if riled, I can temporarily lose the ability to control my own behavior.

The truth is, it's the loss of control that scares me more

than anything. Once you know the embarrassment of acting completely out of character, feeling as if your body was controlled like a marionette by some invisible puppeteer, you are never the same. It is a feeling I have already been introduced to, but will in time become depressingly familiar with.

* * *

There is no definitive test for bipolar disorder. It is diagnosed based on symptoms and the elimination of other causes. Even the symptoms can sometimes be difficult to identify with certainty. There are times when a personality trait or a character flaw is just that and nothing more. It takes a psychiatrist who is also a skilled detective to tease out the truth.

The details of much of my past behavior, such as the context surrounding a dramatic incident, my mindset and moods leading up to it, have been lost to me in the interceding years. Were my angry outbursts a symptom of a yet-to-be diagnosed illness or just another character flaw? Nothing can ever excuse a tirade that has already been had but it might ease some of my guilt and embarrassment if there was at least some explanation for it. Grown men shouldn't have tantrums. Maybe I was just immature. Maybe I just had anger management issues. I'll probably never know for sure. Here, though, is what I do know.

At this time, rage is not listed as an official symptom of bipolar disorder. Perhaps it cannot be agreed upon whether the anger is being caused by the illness or if it is just a common temperament of people who have the illness. It is, however, impossible to ignore the overwhelming number of bipolars who report, to one extent or another, experiencing intense and volatile outbursts of anger.

These outbursts are not normal reactions to provocation. They are irrational. They are disproportionate to the events that precipitate them. They are like wildfires. They can be extremely disruptive and even violent, leading, sometimes to the loss of jobs and interpersonal relationships. Those experiencing the rages usually describe them as frightening and overwhelming. They report feeling out of control or beyond their bodies as if they are watching someone else. Afterward, when the anger has passed, they describe feelings of remorse, confusion, and shame.

The explosiveness and unpredictability of these angry flares can be very upsetting not only to those experiencing them but also to any dear loved ones. None of this should be surprising since bipolar disorder, by its very nature, is an illness characterized by extremes in moods and emotions. It is not uncommon for bipolars to overreact to certain situations or to describe heightened emotional responses to many of their experiences.

Research is also beginning to show that people with bipolar disorder often seem to experience more anger than people either without the disorder or with other mental disorders. Furthermore, they can experience this type of anger even between cycles, when they are neither acutely manic nor depressed. So there's that.

# Chapter 18

# You Think I'm What?

Another interesting hiccup occurs in early 1996. My wife is pregnant with our first child and I decide to leave the hospital where I am working to accept a higher paying position at a company doing insurance case management. I try it for a few months but it's a bust. I hate the job beyond words and no amount of money can convince me to stay.

My first instinct is to return to the hospital that I left and try to get my old job back. The position is still open and considering that I left in good standing and require no training, I expect I will be rehired on the spot. This is not the case though.

After re-applying and hearing nothing back, I contact a close friend who still works there to try and find out what's going on. She tells me that the unit management held a meeting to decide whether or not they wanted to rehire me. After some discussion, they decide it would not be a good idea and reject my application. I am understandably confused by this news and press my friend for the reasons they gave.

She dodges the question but I know she was present during the meeting so I continue to push. Eventually and with great reluctance, she tells me that the manager and assistant manager felt it would be a mistake because in their opinion, I was not mentally stable.

It is like I have been punched in the gut. I turn the words around in my head trying to make them, in some way, apply to me but I can't. I am confused and embarrassed. I have always thought I wasn't quite right but the realization that other people might think so too is mortifying. How could they have seen that in me? I barely even see it in myself anymore. Most of all that stuff is in my past. Isn't it?

I remember now that the very same assistant manager who is my friend took me aside and expressed her concern that I was unstable and might need psychiatric help. I was so shocked at the time that I did not address it at all. I broke off the conversation and stayed away from her after that thinking the problem must be hers. She did not pursue it and I never asked her why she thought so. Eventually, I all but forgot about the incident and things returned to normal. Now it was back again. I had no idea then, nor do I now, what I had done to set off her kookometer. I know only that I no longer want my old job back and hope to God I never see any of my former co-workers again.

I wrap up the conversation with my friend in a hurry. I ask for no clarification or further details. I wish her the best and hang up as quickly as I can. I sit by the phone in silence several long minutes trying to process what I have been told but I have no luck. Imagining what the people in that meeting must have said about me makes me feel ill. All that I take from the incident is that my own assessment of my behavior cannot be relied upon. I will have to be more vigilant about censoring my thoughts and feelings from others.

# Chapter 19

# Off To the Races

One of the advantages of being a nurse is that there are always plenty of job opportunities. It is not long before I secure another position and move on with my life. I will remain in this job for seven long and happy years. It is at the hospital where, although I don't know it yet, I will one day be a psychiatric patient.

It is around September of 1998 and I am enjoying my work and a new role at home, father. My daughter Cornelia is just over a year old and the two of us are inseparable. My life after years of awkward stumbling seems finally to have gained its footing. Things are good. I've found my stride. Keeping it will prove to be the challenge.

The trouble begins stealthily with a gradual elevation in my mood. My energy level is up and everything seems to be going my way. I work from 5:30 a.m. till 2:00 p.m. I go to the gym after work, then pick up Cornelia from day care and the two of us spend the afternoon together. I have no worries.

Perhaps the first noticeable change in my behavior is my reading habits. I am always reading a book. I read before bed and while eating my lunch at work. I read in waiting rooms and on the pot. When I am done with one book, I return it to the library and pick up another to start the same day. One book at a time, never any hurry. I have been doing this as long as I can remember. Now, however, it is becoming difficult, no impossible, to stick to a single book.

The length of my trips to the library first doubles then triples. So many interesting titles. I read the jacket blurb on one book and am hooked in an instant. Instead of heading to the check-out desk, though, I continue browsing. My eyes move hungrily from one spine to the next. I slide each one from its snug little niche and read its blurb as well. Oh my gosh! This is fascinating! I have to have it. And this one! And this! When I leave the library more than an hour later I am carrying an arm load of books with me to the car. Many I will read from cover to cover. Others I will start but never finish, either running out of time or just losing interest in them.

Despite already having more library books than I can read, I find myself still browsing Barnes & Noble and Half Priced Books a couple of times a week. Half Priced is irresistible. I never leave without a sack of at least half a dozen new books. The side table next to my bed is stacked a foot high with books and the floor next to the bed has two or three more face down and open to mark my current page in each of them.

It is not just the volume of my reading that is ballooning,

but my interest in new subjects as well. I am reading books on such diverse topics as the Nuremburg trials after World War II, the art of Peter Paul Rubens, cooking, music theory, the history of the New York City Ballet, the autobiography of Bo Jackson, the *The Vampire Chronicles* by Anne Rice, *The Hitchhiker's Guide to the Galaxy* by Douglas Adams, a book about the Philadelphia Experiment, and any fiction that catches my interest: action, crime, survival, drama, you name it. One day something like this will set off alarm bells in my head telling me I may be winding up to a mania, but at this time I'm not even sure what mania is, so with no idea that anything is wrong, I race ahead like a lemming toward a cliff.

At work I become much more outgoing. This is a wonderful new experience for me. I am finally coming out of my shell. It's not like I had been a complete introvert before or anything. I guess I've just always been kind of quiet and bookish. I keep one or two close friends and that's it. I am not good in groups and keep a safe distance from the people I meet on the job. They are acquaintances and co-workers, not friends, but then that was the old me.

Now I find myself opening up to people more and more and enjoying the interaction. In fact, I find the conversation wonderfully stimulating and everyone is suddenly my friend. I am interested in whatever they have to tell me and become utterly absorbed in the minutia of their lives. I question everything, no detail is too small to beguile me.

It seems also, that the gregarious new me is as attractive to other people as they are to me. As a man working in nursing, I have no shortage of good looking female co-workers and I suddenly find flirtatious relationships developing with a number of them. My marriage is not as strong as it once was but I am a committed family man and am not looking to start an affair. Nevertheless, the flirting is a little addictive and I am sort of going to town with it. I am not a man who has been in a position to enjoy this sort of thing much in my life, if ever. It is a soothing balm to my long brutalized self-esteem and the guilty pleasure of it lifts my mood even higher.

I flirt with my boss (always a bad idea), two of the nurses who work with me on my unit, both of whom are married. I flirt with several nurses who work in the OR, then an anesthesiologist and an anesthesia resident. No one seems out of reach. Did I really just say that?

At home things are different too. I am planning home improvements and rearranging furniture left and right. I find there is not enough time during the days to dedicate to my many blossoming interests, but neither can I streamline the list. It is extremely important that I work on them all. For this reason, I mastermind a schedule of activities for my afternoons and draw it out on a sheet of paper. For each activity I allot 30 minutes. When time is up, regardless of where I am, I stop and move on to the next activity.

A typical afternoon now includes: drawing, reading, learning a foreign language, teaching myself to play the keyboard, and practicing my pitching in the backyard. I do this by hurling tennis balls at a chalk outline of a strike zone I have drawn onto our wooden fence. Pitching gets the extra 15 minutes because I decide that if I get good enough, I will try my luck as a walk on for the Texas Rangers. They need some good pitching.

At night after I have put Cornelia to bed I burn up the phone lines calling my friends and family around the state and country. I yammer on about whatever I am feeling excited about that night, which is pretty much everything. I talk about particle physics as if I know something about it, comic books, movies, artists, and art.

I tell my father that I am surprisingly moved by ballet and describe it as the perfect blending of music, athletics, and art. I even tell him that if had I known it would make me feel like this one day I may have tried my hand at it when I was younger. It is so up my alley that I may have been good at it. My father is understandably perplexed by the statements especially since ballet was never up my alley at all until about a month ago.

I tell everyone about the plans I am making to join the National Guard. I pressure my old friend Jeff to partner with me in writing a humorous book that I am certain we can publish and make a fortune. The following day I add working on the book to my daily activity schedule. Over the next two months I will complete more than fifty illustrations for it. I talk to Brian about several money making schemes and to my sister about how achieving all of life's dreams is as simple as putting your mind to it.

I begin to notice more and more that as I talk I am changing topics with dizzying speed. My thoughts are all over the place. I can tell it is exasperating for the people I am talking to, but I find I can't help it. My mind skitters across ideas so quickly that the moment I begin to expound on one, the next two more after that are already there. I elaborate where I can, then go racing after my mind—trying to keep up. Each idea is electrifying, each theory ground breaking, and each joke a breath stealer. I simply have to share them as fast as they come. I have no patience for remaining on topic.

I begin to feel self-conscious about all these quicksilver changes in my train of thought, not in an, "I might be ill" sort of way, but in a way that tells me I might need to limit the phone calls or conversations I have with the same individuals. I can't keep silent. That's out of the question, but I can keep alternating the people to whom I talk with so that no one person figures out how fast my mind is racing. I don't want anyone to think I am weird. I'm not weird am I? Nah. Not a chance! Weird like a fox, maybe!

At night I am sleeping less. Not significantly less and it's not because I can't sleep. It's just that I am too busy to waste my time sleeping any more than is necessary. Instead of getting my usual eight hours of sleep, something I have been sort of fanatical about through the years, I stay awake reading or making illustrations for my book, or practicing my Spanish. When I do lie down now, there is often only five or so hours left before my alarm goes off. Still, this seems to be more than enough and I am happy to reassign those previously wasted hours to more important pastimes.

When I do close my eyes to sleep I begin to see random unrelated images of things flashing behind my eyelids. This is different than dreaming. There is no sound. There is no story line. Just images flashing by so fast I can scarcely register what one image is before it has changed to something else. I don't know where all the images are coming from. If there is a chain of logic connecting them, I can't see it, and there is no way to block them out. My eyes are already closed. I just ignore them like a movie I'm not really watching and before I know it, I am asleep.

My mind has been steadily accelerating for close to two months now and if anyone has remained unaware of it thus far they are beginning to notice it now. In addition to the racing thoughts and rocket propelled speech I am becoming more impulsive. For my Halloween costume this year I make a Phantom of the Opera mask and excitedly drop a small fortune on a top of the line tuxedo rental. I'm gonna look great though! I also buy art supplies, sheet music, tools and hardware…just stuff. My wife questions all the spending but I brush her off. I'm fine. I've got this.

Spending is not the only thing my wife questions. I am irritable around the house. Whatever I am working on takes on great importance and cannot be interrupted. When it is, my frustration is palpable. When she not as excited about the increasingly flaky plans I am making for my life as I feel she should be, I turn on her accusing her of being boring and without ambition. I am snappy and rude. I am an ass. I tell her that we are not a good couple anymore because the truth is that she just can't keep up with me. It makes no sense but I mean every word of it when I say it. She is nervous around me now and getting to the point where she doesn't know how to handle me.

At work I am still talking to everyone but have moved beyond listening. Listening interferes with my talking. I am no longer able to keep my many plans a secret. I am aware that I have always been a person who dreams big, but never follows through so I have developed the habit of keeping my ideas to myself until I make them happen. Personal history has taught me well that answering the question, "Hey, whatever happened to" this plan or that one, gets to be embarrassing. It is better to play my cards close to my chest until I am certain that I am going to see the plan through. I don't like people rolling their eyes at me like they know I'm just all talk.

Now, however, it seems that all my schemes and ambitions are absolute certainties, and I am way too excited to keep any cards close to my chest. I tell anyone who will listen, and quite a few people who won't, all about them in great rambling detail. I drop bizarre trivial facts around like people will have the slightest idea what I'm referring too. I am obnoxious and still at times hilarious. I am so distracted that it is getting dangerous for me to work but I can't tell. To me, sickness means fever and I don't have a fever. All must be well.

My mind is all over the place. My pockets are filled with scraps of paper containing snippets of poetry that keep writing themselves in my head, along with sketches, to-do lists, ideas for inventions and notes for things I can't keep up with anymore.

Finally, I start to think something may be off. I'm doing all these new things believing that they're in harmony with the "real me." Are they though? Or are they just strange and out of character? Like suddenly listening to all kinds of classical music, something I couldn't have cared less about a couple of months ago. What am I doing? Am I finding myself, or losing my mind?

I have a stack of new CDs of Beethoven, Bach, Debussy, and Schumann. I have even bought a couple of books on the lives of the great composers. I can't seem to keep track of my own plans anymore. Is everything of the utmost importance or is it all meaningless crap? I am getting confused and forgetful, and worst of all, I can't seem to shut the hell up. For the first time since this upswing began, I begin to feel scared. For the first time, I realize that there is something very wrong with me.

## Chapter 20

# You Can't Be Serious

The hospital where I am working has an Employee Assistance Program or EAP. This is a benefit for the employees, sort of free temporary therapy for problems that arise such as grief, domestic problems, depression, or anything else that might be affect an employee's ability to do their job. I would never have imagined that I would take advantage of it but I am so alarmed at my increasingly odd behavior and my inability to control it that I stow my embarrassment and call the number anyway. They schedule an appointment for me in a couple of days. I don't know what I will say to the therapist. How do you talk to a therapist? I have no idea what's wrong with me. I only know that I am not myself.

At the appointment I am met in the lobby by a slightly creepy looking guy wearing a pair of thick glasses from the 1970s. He's a little paunchy and dressed in corduroy pants. Lately my ability to see patterns and interesting relationships seems to be heightened and on seeing this guy, it occurs to me that **t-h-e-r-a-p-i-s-t** also spells "the rapist." Probably just a coincidence though. He is holding a yellow legal pad and the intake forms which I filled out on arrival. He introduces himself, and leads me back to a quiet office at the end of a hallway. He has a desk in the room but doesn't sit behind it. Instead we sit in a couple of comfortable chairs that look more like they belong in someone's living room than in an office. He asks me what brought me here today and how he can help. His manner seems surprisingly caring and sincere and I consider that perhaps my initial aversion to him had more to do with his profession than him. And the glasses. Probably the glasses too.

Deciding to give him a chance, I start to try and explain but make an awful mess of it. My descriptions are all over the place and I talk too fast. Everything comes out in jumble. I tell him that I'm not myself and that I can't keep up with my thoughts and plans. I try to explain to him about my focus darting all over the place. How I'm afraid I've been making a fool of myself by talking maybe a bit too excitedly to friends, family and co-workers about just about everything and I can't stop it.

The therapist nods but doesn't comment. It's like he's still waiting for me to tell him why I'm here. None of what I'm telling him is getting my point across. It all sounds vague and trivial when I say it. I rub my face with my hands in frustration. I recall a children's story I once heard as a kid. I hadn't thought of the story in years but it comes back to me now and kind of strikes a chord. I look at the therapist, take a breath, and try again. I tell him the story.

It was the story of a boy who wanted to dance at an upcoming festival in his village in order to impress a girl he liked. Unfortunately, he didn't know how to dance so he asked a witch for help. The witch agreed to help him and gave the boy a pair of magic shoes. The boy went to the festival and put on the shoes. Just as the witch had promised, he began to dance and found he could do it amazingly well. He was thrilled and let the shoes take him to new places. He whirled and spun and leaped and turned cartwheels. No one could take their eyes off him and they all clapped for him—even the girl.

When he was finished and tried to stop he found that he couldn't. Instead, he only danced faster. He danced and danced, exhausted and unable to stop himself, faster and faster until everyone got scared and ran away. He danced through the night and into the next day, terrified and out of control.

I sigh. "I can't remember how it ended," I say. "You know, if he ever got the shoes off or not." I look at the therapist miserably. "It's kind of like that though," I say and to my surprise, find tears beginning to well in my eyes. Great. I blink them back and take a deep breath. The therapist waits for me to regain control. "Sorry," I say after a moment. "I just don't know what's going on with me lately."

I don't know what I expected to happen today but it sure wasn't this. The therapist talks kindly to me. His voice is quiet and reassuring. I am immensely relieved that he is doing the talking now instead of me. He tells me there's someone he'd like me to talk to, a doctor. He says this doctor can help me and asks my permission to call him. He wants to tell him about me and see if we can arrange an appointment. For some reason he thinks it's important that I get seen right away.

I tell him okay and watch as he picks up the phone right there in front of me. When he reaches the doctor, he summarizes what I have told him. I hear him say that I have no previous diagnosis of bipolar disorder. I remember bipolar disorder from my psych rotation in nursing school, what they used to call manic-depressive illness. But that doesn't fit. I know I've been depressed a lot in my life, for most of it really. But that's it, just depressed. And clearly that's not the problem right now.

The problem is I don't know what I'm doing. It's like someone else has hijacked my mind and is living their life with my body. But it isn't me! I mean if you lose control of yourself, you should just stop, right? Become frozen in place, unable to speak or move. That would make sense. Your body shouldn't continue to walk around, talking and doing things all on its own, things you would never say or do…acting in ways you would never act, embarrassing the shit out of you, should it? But that's what's happening. That's the problem!

He nods his head as he answers several questions glancing at me to make sure I have not leapt up and sprinted out of his office. The doctor is saying something to him and he gives me a conformational nod. I want to sprint out his office. There is another pause as the doctor on the other end of the line presumably checks his calendar for his next availability. It will probably be a month off.

The therapist asks me if I am available tomorrow morning at 10:00. Whoa. Tomorrow is Saturday. Do psychiatrists see patients on Saturdays? I tell him I am available and he relays it back to the doctor. After a few more words, he thanks him and hangs up.

"Great news," he tells me. "He can meet with you at his office tomorrow morning at 10:00." He writes the doctor's name and office address on a yellow Post-it note along with his telephone number and 10:00 a.m.

Talking to an EAP therapist is one thing but an actual psychiatrist? After one visit? I was right. There is something wrong with me, isn't there? Shit. Am I crazy? I take the Post-it feeling sort of numb. The therapist gives me some words of encouragement and makes me promise to keep the appointment tomorrow. I tell him I will and leave the office in a fog. That night it takes me a long time to fall asleep. And when I close my eyes I see swirling colors so intense and overly saturated that I can think of nothing else.

The next morning, I meet Dr. Howard at his office at 10:00 a.m. He is a gentle man, sort of effeminate, with a nonjudgmental and competent air about him. I dislike him at once.

He does nothing to deserve it. I just don't want to need him for anything. I don't want to be part of his world. I want to be part of my world, the world of my friends and family, mowing my grass, laughing over beers, playing with my daughter, and watching baseball on TV. Not the world of effeminate psychiatrists, not the world of drama, and certainly not the world of lying around on a shrink's couch inside on a beautiful Saturday in autumn to whine about my life.

Since I was a kid, one of my greatest heroes was Chuck Yeager, the fearless Air Force test pilot and first man to fly faster than sound. Chuck would never have to go and see a psychiatrist. I clench my jaw irritably because of the vast incalculable differences that exist between Chuck Yeager and myself. And because deep down, I know I really need to be here. I know it. So instead of getting out and enjoying my Saturday, instead of telling Dr. Howard that this has all been a mistake, I sit here in another office, hating myself and hating Dr. Howard.

Dr. Howard's office is arranged similarly to the EAP therapist's office that I visited yesterday only this place stinks of money. He has an immense mahogany desk, probably once owned by Andrew Carnegie or something, the ubiquitous couch against one wall, two exquisitely upholstered armchairs, and a built in floor-to-ceiling bookcase that spans an entire wall full of thick leather-bound books with gilded lettering on their spines. There are tasteful abstract paintings on the walls and a couple of sculptures on the shelves that look like they each cost a year of my salary. And of course there is a breathtaking view of the city through the enormous window beside his desk.

It seems a bit much to me. Like maybe you should be a little more low key when you are making your money off the suffering of others. I know this is not fair. He makes it off easing the suffering of others, a huge difference, but it might be easier to see him that way if his office was a little less flashy.

Despite my feelings toward him, Dr. Howard proves to be patient and kind. He is professional, knowledgeable, and gives me the grudging confidence that I have done the right thing in coming here. I do my best to explain to him what has been happening to me. I answer his questions and try my best not to ramble but I am scattered and have trouble focusing. I keep getting away from the subject.

Sometimes trying to lighten the mood, I joke and guffaw maybe a bit too explosively. I think the jokes are funny, but he just smiles politely so I have my doubts. He nods his head and takes notes. Nothing I say seems to surprise him. He asks me about my sleep patterns, about my spending, and about my family history. He is thorough and unhurried. We talk for well over and hour. When he is satisfied, he delivers his verdict.

I stare, disbelieving as Dr. Howard tells me that I have bipolar disorder. There is no cure for it, and I will need to be on medication for the rest of my life. He is very clear on the medication thing and tells me how dangerous this illness can be. It is not something to be treated lightly he tells me. The price of ignoring bipolar disorder is often a person's marriage, career, or financial security. And it tends to get worse if left untreated. Well, that's just splendid news.

"You're familiar with bipolar disorder?" Dr. Howard asks.

I nod, lost for the moment, for words. I look out the window. At last I manage a weak, "I mean I guess." My voice is flat. "Just what we covered in school." He waits for me to continue. "I once interviewed a woman with bipolar during my psych rotation but she seemed pretty normal to me."

He nods, then sets his note pad on the desk and shifts a little in his fabulous chair. He inhales slowly through his nose as though gathering his thoughts, then he hits the high points for me. "Bipolar is a mood disorder characterized by extremes in mood, alternating patterns of highs and lows sometimes with healthy periods in between." He takes a deep breath and licks his teeth.

"In a manic phase, a person might experience excesses in energy with a decreased need for sleep. Their speech may become rapid and pressured. Thoughts can race, a phenomenon known as a 'flight of ideas.' They might take self-indulgent activities to excess such as spending large amounts of money or having casual sexual encounters without concern for the consequences. Other symptoms could include unrealistic or grandiose beliefs in one's abilities. A person may even become delusional believing they are famous or have special powers. As the mania progresses, they can become confused, paranoid, or irritable. In rare cases they can even become violent."

He pauses. "Have you ever experienced any of these things?" I don't answer. For the first time in weeks, I don't feel like talking so he continues.

"In a depressive phase a person will probably experience decreased energy sometimes to the point of being unable to work or even leave their bed. They may be unable to enjoy activities that were previously enjoyable to them. They commonly experience feelings of guilt and worthlessness. They may become preoccupied with thoughts of death or suicide. The person may complain of feeling slowed down in their thinking and speech. They might withdraw from friends and family, experience changes in sleep patterns and or appetite."

I notice that Dr. Howard talks smoothly without breaks, like he has given this lecture dozens of times to dozens of patients. He gestures with his hands as he talks. I feel like I'm watching an expert guest on a TV show. I feel a little bit like I'm on a TV show myself. One where they ambush the guest with news that his spouse is sleeping with his best friend or something. It feels that unreal.

"In both phases, concentration, insight and judgment can become severely impaired leading to poor choices. As a result, it is not unusual for people with bipolar illness to find themselves dealing with legal issues, lost jobs, divorces, financial difficulties, sexually transmitted diseases, or substance abuse issues." He pauses, at last, and studies me, giving me a chance to ask questions. I'm still not ready to speak.

"The good news," he goes on to say, "is that, in most cases, it is a very treatable illness. There are a number of good medicines out there that can be quite effective in controlling the symptoms." He smiles as if this will soften the blow that he has just dealt me. It doesn't. All I hear is that I am no longer normal. I mean I've always known it but now it's official. I am defective. I am weak. I am from now on, oh man, mentally ill. Shit shit shit shit shit.

Before I leave Dr. Howard's office he writes me a prescription for Depakote. I recognize the medicine but only know it as an anti-seizure medication. He informs me that several of the anti-seizure medications are now proving successful in the treatment of bipolar disorder as well. It should, over the next two to three weeks, be able to slow my mind back down and get me to feeling and functioning more like myself again. It can, however, be a little hard to metabolize so I will need to have my blood drawn every so often to make sure it is not damaging my liver. Uh huh. He goes on to tell me that he'll need to see me again in two weeks unless I need him sooner. I will need to call his office Monday to schedule my next appointment. And that's it. Just like that.

# Chapter 21

# Swept Under the Rug

Having a doctor tell me that I have a mental illness that will require medication for the rest of my life to control is a peculiar thing. In a way it is not a surprise. It legitimizes something I have suspected for years. I always felt that I had to fake normalcy. Could never understand why I am the way I am. In another way, though, it shocks me. Whatever has been the matter with me all these years, bipolar disorder is the last thing I would have guessed. Trying to get my mind around it is no easy task.

In nursing school I learned about something called a body image disturbance. It refers to the struggle a person undergoes trying to adjust the way he sees himself in the face of a life- changing illness or injury. Some circumstances that might create such a disturbance are obvious like losing a limb or becoming paralyzed. Physical trauma, however, is not the only kind of change that might precipitate a body image disturbance.

Many illnesses such as heart disease, high blood pressure,

or diabetes can also require a difficult adjustment. A person with an illness such as these knows they are no longer like everyone else even it is not obvious to others. Once they are diagnosed they are no longer healthy by the strictest definition. They will, from that point on, probably require medications to function normally. They will be dependent, at least to an extent, on doctors and the health care system.

While the changes to the lives of people diagnosed with high blood pressure or diabetes may be minor compared to those required by a person who has become paralyzed, their psychological impact is not insignificant. People making the adjustment know they can never again go back to the way things were. Their lives are forever different. It is this realization that forces an ultimate acceptance. For me, I discover first hand that the diagnosis of mental illness also requires its own unique and frustratingly difficult adjustment. My true acceptance of the condition will not come for many years.

In the weeks following my visit to Dr. Howard's office not much changes on my surface. I take my medicine as prescribed, against Dr. Howard's advice I continue to work, and my mind continues to race. On the inside though I am ashamed of myself. Being diagnosed with a mental illness is irrefutable proof that I don't measure up. I have difficulty looking people in the eye, especially other men. Men, I assume, have it all together. They, unlike me, are not troubled by such weakness.

I feel like an even bigger fake than usual because everyone continues to talk to me as if were equals. Allowing them to go on thinking this is nothing short of deception. I am a liar, a fraud. Only I know the disgraceful truth.

I am medicated and struggling to not ramble. I still have a pocketful of ideas and half-written poetry scribbled on paper towels, Post-it notes, and other scraps of paper. I am fidgety as hell. I am still having difficulty following what people are saying. I am still wearing a pair of fucking magic shoes that no one can see.

When I talk to my co-workers I make a herculean effort to appear as though I am listening. I nod and force eye contact with them. I look intent and thoughtful, at least I hope that I do. And above all else, I do not allow myself to speak unless absolutely necessary. This is key. The fact that I am able to do it is a good sign. If I get started, though, it's like a flood and I almost have to slam my hand over my mouth to stop.

I make up excuses to the people who I know I weirded out recently. I casually mention that I have had to cut back on coffee because I have been drinking way too much. I tell them it makes me wired and overly talkative. I laugh and they nod a bit suspiciously, but little by little they seem to accept this explanation as long as I continue holding my shit together.

At home I restrict myself from the phone. I have embarrassed myself enough for now. I still work feverishly at a number of activities and manage to complete none of them, but slowly the medicine begins to seep into my brain like cold molasses. It slows down the wildly spinning gears. By Thanksgiving I feel more in control. My liver function tests look normal and I feel optimistic that I'll soon have this thing licked.

As my ability to concentrate on a single activity for longer than a few minutes improves, I decide to begin reading up on this thing they say I have. Know your enemy, right? I go back to the library, my haven. In addition to what Dr. Howard outlined to me at his office, I learn that bipolar disorder occurs along a spectrum that can range from pretty manageable in some cases to very severe.

At its worst, it can be devastating. It can ruin people's lives and become completely disabling. It can confound psychiatrists and defy all attempts to control its symptoms or slow its course. In these cases, it can result in serial hospitalizations, extended care, and suicide.

On the other hand, there are less severe versions of the disorder with symptoms that are deceptively vague. Many people on the milder end of the spectrum go undiagnosed and unmedicated their entire lives because none of their symptoms are severe enough for them to even realize they are ill. They struggle at times with difficulties they simply consider normal for them or at least are only intermittently troubling. One thing is certain: bipolar disorder can be experienced in almost as many ways as there are people who experience it.

For general purposes, a number of accepted points along the bipolar spectrum have been named and categorized by the oft-cited Diagnostic Statistical Manual of Mental Disorders. These are called the bipolar subtypes and are summarized as follows: **Bipolar I**—Severe manias alternating with severe depressions. This is the most brutal form of the illness. **Bipolar II**—Severe depression and hypomanias with normal periods in between. Hypomania is a less severe form of mania. **Cyclothymia**—Mild depressions with hypomanias and normal periods. Cyclothymic episodes are usually milder and shorter in duration than those of Bipolar I or II. **Rapid Cycling**—Defined as experiencing at least four episodes of either depression or mania within a 12-month period. And **Bipolar Not Otherwise Specified**—Sort of a catch all subtype intended to lump together all the other subtle variations of the illness that do not fit cleanly into the other subtypes.

I read about medication treatments for bipolar. I read about the antidepressants, the neuroleptics, and the mood stabilizers. About the importance of taking medications as prescribed and not stopping them unless instructed to by my psychiatrist. I read about the importance of getting enough sleep, how not getting enough of it can trigger either mania or depression. I read about the destabilizing effects of stress, alcohol and drugs and how they also can contribute to episodes in people with bipolar disorder. And I read first-hand accounts of experiences from people with the illness. None of it is very encouraging, though nearly all of it tries to be. In the end, I put away all the books and just push it, as much as possible, out of my mind.

By Christmas I am back to my old self, for whatever that is worth. I am still in a honeymoon period with my medication. I credit it with my return to sanity and control. I am looking people in the eye again and smugly thinking to myself, I am just like you, thanks to Depakote. The shock of diagnosis has worn off and the bad memories are fading.

Friends and family already seem to be forgetting my bizarre behavior and I am happy to join them in the fantasy. In order to help speed things along, I collect anything and everything that reminds me of my "little episode" and throw it all away.

I throw out the drawings and sketches I made while manic, my recently purchased books and CDs, I throw out my poems and the random articles I clipped from magazines on this topic or that. All the things I researched while on lightning impulse. I return a mountain of books to the library. I put my keyboard and all my art supplies into the attic where they'll be out of sight and the almost consuming frenzy of passion they brought about in me can be forgotten.

I return an opaque projector to the store that I bought during yet another dazzling flash of inspiration. The plan had been to use it to paint a mural, a la Sistine Chapel, on the wall over my fireplace. Probably wouldn't have gone over well with my wife anyway.

I scour the house and garage for all the ill-advised projects that are still scattered here and there in various stages of incompleteness and either toss or dismantle them. When I am finished, no evidence remains. I wash my hands of it all. I've always been good at denial.

The trouble with a cyclic mood disorder is that once an episode has passed it begins to seem as though it never happened at all. How could it have? Maybe I jumped the gun going to see a psychiatrist, I tell myself. Maybe I made more of it than there was. I was probably just excited. Fall has always been my favorite season. Surely I could have controlled myself better if I had really put my mind to it. And psychiatrists…well of course they're gonna say I'm sick. They're always trying to hang labels on folks. It's how they make their money right? I feel fine. There's no way I'm bipolar. Dr. Howard is one who's crazy. This was a mistake.

It is at this point that so many people with bipolar disorder stop taking their meds, setting up their eventual and inevitable relapse. I keep taking my Depakote though. I guess it can't hurt. It doesn't seem to be bothering my liver and it's not a bad idea to cover my bases, right? You know, just in case.

Dr. Howard scared me pretty good with some of his stories about his other bipolar patients. He wanted to drive home the point about how serious it could be if I don't attend to it, the damage I could do to my life if I were to temporarily go out of my head. It worked. Although I am more and more certain, the longer I feel normal, that there is nothing wrong with me, I still hear a tiny voice inside me that says, yeah, but what if…what if… what if Dr. Howard is right?

It's too sketchy to risk ditching the medication, at least right now, so I keep taking it. I keep my periodic appointments. I sleep when I'm supposed to. I exercise when I can, and life returns to normal, Well, a new normal anyway, but what the hell. Close enough.

People are funny. When we need somebody and when we're scared, we will often turn to those who can help us change, chameleon-like, into whatever or whoever they need us to be in order to get help. We will make whatever promises we need to, agree to almost anything, and even believe it all ourselves.

Once the crisis has past and Jack is back in his box, all is forgotten. It's business as usual. We can rationalize any responsibility away and conveniently forget whatever suits us now that we are no longer desperate and afraid. Man, are we ever shits. God must just roll his eyes at all the deathbed pledges he has had to listen to through the centuries.

As for me, I sought help from the mental health care system when I was panicked and out of control. I was honest with them. I accepted them and their profession, albeit grudgingly. I needed them and was grateful for their help. I even told myself that I accepted my diagnosis and would go quietly to flock together with birds of my own feather. But as my life returns from the brink, I become as anxious to discard my saviors as I had been to discard my art, poetry, and projects. They are all reminders of what I need to forget and to deny.

As months become years, blame and resentment for the incident become so distilled around Dr. Howard that I can taste it in my mouth. I can't stand going to my appointments anymore. Even sitting in his waiting area is becoming unbearable. I beg him to space out my appointments as long as possible, reassuring him that I am doing fine.

Day to day, I don't even remember that I have a psychiatric diagnosis. I am normal and healthy. My medication is totally unnecessary and I am only continuing to take it as a favor to my wife. Also as a sort of insurance policy in the unlikely event there is a recurrence, another perfect alignment of environmental, professional, and dietary factors that must have been present in the autumn of 1998 to cause me to become a little…let's just call it flighty. I am content and life is proceeding satisfactorily. Then each time I have to return to Dr. Howard s office for a follow-up, everything is thrown back in my face again. It's maddening!

In time, the hospital I am working for changes its employee insurance provider and Dr. Howard is no longer covered under my plan. Wonderful! I am so thrilled that I will never have to return to that man's office that after my last appointment, I lay a scratch in the parking lot as I leave and spray a shower of gravel behind me.

I enjoy more than six blissful months of psychiatrist-free living until my last refill of Depakote runs low and I am forced to find a new doctor. I choose a female psychiatrist within the hospital system where I work. It's a little risky but her office is in another building several blocks away from the hospital. I doubt I will run in to anyone I know there.

Dr. Wentz is attractive but not intimidating. She is simple and I like her far more than Dr. Howard. No bad memories. She has never seen me crazy. My history is just words in a file. I feel safer talking to a female as well. I always think a man is going to judge me more harshly.

There is no truth in this. Deep down I know it is only because I would judge another man more harshly. I have been unable to let of go of the belief that mental illness is a sign of weakness and a man must never be weak. The fact that I can recognize this judgmental aspect of my character doesn't make it any easier to let go of it. It just spotlights another of my flaws. I'll work on that later though. For now I just make a mental note to select exclusively female psychiatrists whenever possible.

Dr. Wentz's office is small and unassuming. I like that too. It is as simple as she is. There is a loveseat in place of a couch on one wall. I sit here. A couch wouldn't t fit in such a small office. A utilitarian reading chair sits near the loveseat facing it at a nonthreatening angle. She sits here. A small end table separates the two with a couple of magazines and a potted ivy. There is a small cheap desk, particle board with fake oak laminate, sticking out from the other wall with a phone, a picture frame, several stacks of scattered file folders, and a table lamp.

Dr. Wentz never uses the overhead light during our appointments, only the lamp. That way the office always seems dim and intimate. For some reason the low light makes me feel anonymous like I'm in a Catholic confessional. I like it, and for a time anyway, going there is a tolerable periodic interruption to my otherwise un-mentally ill life.

# Chapter 22

# A New Beginning

I begin 2003 by ending my 13-year marriage. My wife and I have struggled since our daughter was born five years earlier, growing farther and farther apart by degrees until there is nothing left to save. There is plenty of blame to go around but in the end, it is me who hammers down the final nail in the coffin of our relationship and she who files for the divorce. The marriage wasn't a mistake. We weren't wrong. We were just young. I'm surprised that any marriages at all survive the immaturity of youth or the changes that happen as we grow up and grow apart. What the hell do we know in our early twenties about choosing a partner for life anyway?

After only a year, I am again ready to climb back into the marital saddle with a co-worker named Faith. Faith and I have shared a years-long simmering attraction to one another that finally ignited. She is exotically beautiful and sweet and I have fallen for her like a steel worker off a thirty story I-beam. I know I will ask her to marry me but before

I can propose, I'll have to confess the dark secret of my alleged bipolar disorder. By now, in my mind it has become alleged and nothing more, something in my opinion that no longer even needs medicating.

One night over a quiet dinner at my house, I broach the subject with Faith. To both my surprise and delight, the revelation doesn't seem to concern her at all. Of course I describe it as benignly as I can, dismissing it with a wave of my hand, the whole thing a big misunderstanding.

She asks me about what had happened and how I had been diagnosed. I give her a watered down version of the events, smirking and rolling my eyes as if nothing could be more absurd. Of course I have my own explanations for what led to that strange autumn, things such as job burn-out, stress, and some kind of seasonal mood swing.

I tell her that I believe my diagnosis was an error, which I do, and my medication a useless precaution. My doctor, being in the business of labeling people, understandably jumped to conclusions. That's all. I don't hold it against him. But who knows more, a board certified psychiatrist, or me? Exactly. Right? Should I accept whatever he tells me simply because he's been to medical school? No way. I'm not some buck-toothed rube. I think I know what's going on in my own head for Christ's sake.

The only reason I have been taking my medicine all these years, I continue, was to appease my ex-wife's fears. And although I didn't believe the diagnosis, I do have a young daughter. I didn't want to be wrong about this thing and wind up putting her in danger somehow. Bipolars can lose all their judgment during an episode. Up till now, I hadn't wanted to take the risk of stopping my meds however small I considered that risk to be.

Things are different now, I explain cautiously testing the ice. Avoiding an argument with my ex is no longer a concern. My daughter Cornelia is now sadly only visiting me instead of living with me every day, so she is less likely to be caught up in any nonsense if something were to happen. If there were ever a time that I could roll the dice and bet on the fact that I'm right and not Dr. Howard or his ridiculous alarmist diagnosis this, by golly, is it!

I look into Faith's dark eyes and search them for apprehension but find none. My confidence buoyed, I make the final push. I tell Faith that I'm so sure I'm okay that, more than anything, I would like to stop my meds. Still, I tell her, I won't do it if she thinks it's a mistake.

She smiles without hesitation, hugs me, and tells me she loves me. She says it makes no difference to her if I am bipolar or not. Whatever I want to do concerning my health and medication is okay with her. If I truly think it is a misdiagnosis and want to stop my meds she will support me all the way. At the same time, if after doing so she notices any increasingly strange behavior on my part she will bring it to my attention. We can do whatever is necessary at that time to get me taken care of and back on meds. To her, having bipolar disorder is nothing to be embarrassed of even if I have it. It would be no different than my having high cholesterol or whatever else. Wow!

She goes on to make a confession that she has suffered

recurrent bouts of depression for most of her adult life and is currently on medication herself. Just a little something to help keep her on solid ground. It's this experience I realize that makes her able to take my news so easily in stride. Mood disorders, psychiatrists, and psych meds are already all familiar to her. I am not concerned about taking care of her should she become depressed. I have spent so much of my life in that state of mind that I figure I am uniquely qualified for the job. So neither of us sees the other's psychiatric issues as a problem. Instead we simply assume our love will conquer all.

That very day, I drop both my Depakote and my next appointment card for the psychiatry clinic into the trash. I am liberated! I am myself again. Healthy. Happy. Normal. There are no skeletons in my closet or in my medicine cabinet. I dance a little jig.

In July of 2004 Faith and I are married. It is a second marriage for both of us. Faith comes to it with a son, August who is 11, and a daughter, Sadie who is four, from her first marriage and I come with Cornelia from mine who has just turned seven. Though our kids attend the wedding ceremony, the specter of mental illness does not. I have left it behind, already forgotten. It is just a part of my past, discarded like my old retainer and head gear from high school. As for our marriage, I am old enough this time to understand the full weight of the commitment I am making. I vow to stand behind it this time and make it work. I already have one divorce on my record. I promise myself I will not have a second.

# Chapter 23

# Quirky

The first year off medication glides happily by without incident. I am vindicated. Still, I don't put mental illness completely out of mind. A year is convincing evidence on my behalf but it is not definitive yet I suspect. Time though, as is its nature, passes. One year turns into two and then three. Now we're talking. I knew it all along! Misdiagnosed. Ahhh, well. It's all behind me now, meaningless.

My temper resurfaces a few times but I'm sure it's unrelated. Just adjustment issues getting the better of me of Faith and me learning to live together. The first years of marriage can be both passionate as well as challenging. Everyone knows that.

I have changed jobs again and am working at another large university hospital in the city. A couple of times I struggle with what I am disappointed to see is the return of depression, my old and hated foe. I slink back to the doctor and accept treatment on these two occasions. I see a new doctor in each case and never mention my one-time diagnosis of bipolar to either of them. Why cloud the issue with silliness?

I confess nothing more than a long-time history of recurrent depressions that began in adolescence. In each case I take an anti-depressant for about six to nine months until the coast is clear, then toss them away and move on. I'm fine. Doctors are for sick people.

"A tendency toward depression." That is the revised diagnosis that I give myself. No doctors necessary. Not so bad. I have known people who suffer with chronic depression so severe that they cannot stop their medication for even a week without enduring an immediate and vicious recurrence. Not me. I simply have a tendency toward it. It kind of stinks, but it's nothing to be embarrassed about. Once I'm on my feet again I can hold my own without a problem. Look, Ma! No meds!

Depression makes sense to me in a way bipolar never did. It fits with my life experience and, besides, it may be recurrent but it's not chronic or constant. I don't require continuous psychiatric monitoring. I'm not nuts or anything. Now if I was getting manic too from time to time then yeah, okay, maybe. That might be more suggestive of bipolar, but that's just not me.

The problem is that mania, or more accurately hypomania, is not always easy to recognize. Those experiencing it rarely notice it and even more rarely would consider it to be a problem if they did. If not severe, hypomania feels good. It feels deliciously good. In a hypomanic episode, people feel alive and sharp. They feel confident and full of new creative ideas. Life begins to seem full of opportunities just waiting to be taken advantage of. Colors become more vivid. Listening to music becomes an emotional experience felt in one's bones. And not only is hypomania less likely to interfere with a person's ability to function than full blown mania, but it can actually make them extremely productive.

It is easy for a hypomanic person to believe that his energy and enthusiasm is "the real me" and therefore does not belong in a list of bothersome symptoms he may be experiencing. If he seeks help for his moods, he will probably communicate only the depressive symptoms to his healthcare provider. Other times, depending on how it presents, hypomania may be ignored because it seems unrelated. It is mistaken for nothing more than a little irritability or a little trouble sleeping, but again, its presence goes uncommunicated. Because of this, it is not uncommon for bipolar disorder to be first and erroneously diagnosed as uni-polar depression. I am a nurse. I have, at least at some point, studied this shit. I should know better but I don't.

Whatever the reason, things remain invisible to me and I evade the truth for a few more years. I live contentedly, free of the heavy yoke of mental illness that the overzealous Dr. Howard once tried to hang around my neck. I am confident, even smug in the knowledge that the worst I have to fear is an occasional bout of depression.

I focus my energy on real things that actually concern me like taking care of my family, working, fixing the garage door opener, and getting rid of brown spots in my lawn. I can only delude myself for so long, however. In time, I am forced to revise my self-diagnosis yet again.

The first thing I acknowledge is that the appearances of my depressions are becoming somewhat predictable. There is a pattern to them. They creep in on average once a year, on rare occasion twice. If I have to bet on when they will come and settle over me, turning my world gray and loathsome, I would predict the winter, sometime between Christmas and Valentine's Day. They will likely stay between two weeks and two months. Six weeks is average.

I think of them the way I think of the flu. They are miserable but I know they will pass. I am well practiced at being depressed. I am the Tiger Woods of depression. I've been dealing with it my whole life. Even though I want to hide in bed with the sheets pulled over my head, I can still drag myself through the days and fulfill my obligations. I can compensate. It's the way someone with a bad back learns to ignore the pain and go on with his business. What choice is there?

I don't know for sure how long my depressions may have been cycling this way, maybe a long time. It's possible that I didn't note the pattern sooner because I didn't always identify what I was experiencing as depression at all. The presentation of each depression can be so different from the one before it that it boggles the mind. There are so many different variations but I'm learning to spot them.

Sometimes they sneak in masquerading as job burnout, sometimes as marital dissatisfaction. Sometimes I feel sad and other times just numb. Sometimes I feel profoundly apathetic or I might just feel exhausted and think I am run down or physically ill. In the end as the symptoms worsen and others more familiar to me join the parade, I figure it out. Once I've recognized my symptoms for the depression that they are, I can then steel myself to wait it out.

While a pattern of depressions is more suggestive of bipolar than simply recurrent depressions with no pattern, again, it's not enough to point the crazy finger at me. Unipolar depression also can also have seasonal triggers. I could still be safe. What I don't want to do at this point is add any more damning evidence to that what exists and lend more support to Dr. Howard's wild allegations. I don't want to point out to myself, for example, that I am experiencing recurrent periods of mild hypomania as well...and so, quite naturally, I don't

I have spent years building a very convincing defense for myself against having any serious mental illness. In fact, it's so convincing that I have pulled the wool quite effectively over my own eyes. My uncanny talent for self-deception does have its limits.

The problem that it is getting harder to deny that I am, well, a little quirky, let's just say. There are, I am loathe to admit, periods I go through where I become very enthusiastic. I develop sudden passionate ideas and cannot help but act on them. At these times, it becomes impossible for me to contain my excitement. I make plans and share them with my friends and family. I love to brainstorm and become frustrated when people see the ideas as strange or impractical.

When people do get caught up in my fervor, they become confused when my latest obsession vanishes one day. I just lose interest and turn away from it, feeling that everything was a waste of time. I don't understand how I could have believed in something so stupid. All of my passion melts away, as mysteriously as it came, like snow in the noon day sun. It is never as bad as it was in the autumn of 1997 but I realize it may have been going on for most of my adult life.

A few examples of these sudden and white hot passions are as follows: I will climb the seven summits. I will learn physics and write a formula uniting the forces of electricity, magnetism, and gravity. I will teach myself calculus and become a college professor. I will become a chess grand master. I will learn everything there is to learn about wine and purchase a vineyard where I will build a hacienda and begin producing my own fine wines. I will solve the mystery of Edward Leedskalnin's Coral Castle by reading everything he ever wrote. I will buy a grand piano and learn to play it so beautifully that it will bring tears to people's eyes. I will have a copy of a beautiful Renaissance painting by some Italian master tattooed on my back. I will learn Japanese and move to Tokyo. I will become a novelist and move temporarily to Venice in order to conduct research. And the ole favorite, I will quit my job and become an artist, building a small workshop/gallery in my backyard where I will spend all my time painting and sculpting. Is quirky a good word?

As I begin to recall these periods and countless others like them, I see a similar pattern to the one my depressions follow. I usually have these hot passions, or manias, at least one period a year, but sometimes two. They could last anywhere from a week to a couple of months, and if I had to try and pin down a time when I might expect one, it would be in the fall…like the fucking fall of 1998. Oh man, I can't believe it. I've been doing this all along.

The most discouraging thing about this is that if this whole bipolar thing turns out to be true then the times when I have felt the best in my life, times when I felt I was my truest self…may not have been real. My identity has in many ways revolved around these periods of intense exuberance. Whenever I am not feeling like an utter failure, I secretly believe I have unlimited potential, that I can accomplish almost anything I set my mind to. The only problem, in my view, has been that I can't keep my mind set on any one thing long enough to achieve the greatness which I sporadically dream I am capable of. My dreams are forever coming and going, first too many and then none at all.

To me, the times when my interest and ambition evaporate…that's the sickness talking (if there is one). Maybe it's depression. I don't know but that's what's limiting me. Bipolar, however, suggests that the exuberance itself may be the sickness as well, or at least part of it. Those boring in-between times without my lightning enthusiasms and passions may actually be the "real me." What if I'm not a potential genius? What if I'm just a normal guy with a mental illness? What if that bastard Dr. Howard was right all along?

One evening at home, I am stretched out with a book

in my reading chair. I take a short break from the novel I am reading and turn it face down on my lap. It is then that I happen to notice the curious variety of books on my book shelf. I am slowly coming to grips with the idea that my bipolar diagnosis may not have been quite as far off the mark as I had hoped. I'm not rushing into this revelation though. I'm taking my time. I am struck tonight however by the clear evidence of a hypomanic mind at work expressed along the spines of the many books packed onto the shelves beside me.

As I enjoy fiction, it is not surprising to see this genre taking up the bulk of the space. In addition to fiction there are smaller sections of classics, religion, home improvement, travel, a handful of non-fiction books, and a few self-help books. Nothing out of the ordinary.

Then there are the books that make you go, hmm. The books that just don't fit in. Books that I see now map the fleeting enthusiasms of my rather kaleidoscopic mind. There is a book written in Spanish, a book on Kung Fu, one on Qigong, books of poetry, several books on calculus and discrete mathematics (whatever that is), several more on physics including a college textbook I got assuming that I would easily be able to skip right to the college level. There is a book on learning to speak French (for when I buy my vineyard in the south of France obviously) and a bunch more that I simply bought during a tornado of mental activity, for reasons known not even to myself, and never bothered to read. I just shake my head.

As evidence of an unstable mind, it may be somewhat

inconclusive but considering that there is no definitive test for bipolar, I think a person's bookshelf might be as diagnostically significant as the next thing, maybe more so. I say, show me the bookshelves of fifty people and I'll bet I can spot any manic depressives in the group.

Okay, I make up my mind. It seems I was premature in dismissing my first psychiatrist as a crack pot. My personality type may in fact have an origin somewhere along the bipolar spectrum, but it is not serious enough to bother labeling and it certainly does not interfere with my functioning enough to warrant medicating. What I decide to concede at this point, in regards to my high and low tide moods, is that I am perhaps bipolar*ish*. For now.

## Chapter 24

# Mixed Episode

Doctors say that if left untreated, bipolar symptoms will tend to become worse over time. As I have not paid attention to anything doctors have said thus far, it seems pointless to start now. But beginning around late February and March of 2011 a depression moves in that suggests, not so subtly, that I rethink this tactic.

It begins as a combination of apathy and job burnout. Work becomes difficult and the days begin to seem impossibly long. I withdraw from my patients and co-workers alike. I just don't feel like talking. I get my work done but that's all I can manage and it takes everything I've got.

As the depression deepens, I find myself becoming sensitive to light and sound. Everything becomes so jangly and harsh. Standing beneath an overhead light feels like standing in an icy downpour. I squint my eyes and round my shoulders against the weight of it but it's no use.

I start to avoid direct light wherever I can. When I walk through the hospital, I stay to the side of the hallways, so far to the side, in fact, that my shoulder brushes against the walls as I walk. I don't want to pass directly below any of the fluorescent lights in the ceiling. I can't bear to feel the freezing shock of the light down my collar. Can't stand to have it reflect off of me and make me visible.

Likewise, sound becomes a torment, the speech of those around me, the ringing of phones. It is not physically painful but painful in some strange psychological way I cannot explain. Sound has become noise and it doesn't enter my ears as vibration to be processed into information; it tears into my brain like cold splinters of glass. I cringe from it.

Sounds that should each have their own individual volumes, all blend into one obnoxious noise and it's crashing and clanging and entirely too much. Things happening across the room seem as loud as things happening right next to me. I've heard people who are hard of hearing complain that their hearing aids make the world sound like this too, all jumbled up and all at once. The intensity is so unpleasant that they prefer to turn off their hearing aids just to escape the clamor.

I wish there was something I could turn off but there's nothing I can do. It just stays on all the time. When people talk to me, they see the strain on my face as I try to separate their voices from the background. They ask me if I have a headache. I lie and tell them I do. It's easier than the truth. I'm depressed again and it's getting bad.

It is neither surprising nor very long before this strengthening depression begins to affect my job performance. After nearly twenty years in nursing, I begin to experience anxiety about my professional abilities. I feel like an imposter, constantly afraid I will be exposed. I fear my patients will choke or seize or go into some lethal arrhythmia and I will not know what to do to help them. I fear I will be fired for incompetence—fear I will be put in charge and ruin everything.

My hands start to shake so badly it's almost impossible for me to start an IV, a skill at which I normally excel. My success rate plummets. I am like a golfer who has lost his swing.

My focus is slipping as well. It takes me twice as long to get through the computer charting screens I have been using every day for years. Everything is going to pieces.

One day around mid-morning while in a patient's room, I experience a sort of inexplicable freak out. A sense of overwhelming dread and intense restlessness grips me. I feel like I can't continue working. I can't think straight. My heart starts pounding in my chest. I don't know if I'm sick or if I may finally be going crazy.

I flee from the room and retreat, almost running, to the nurses' station and collapse into a chair in a corner hoping to go unseen. I turn toward the wall and start biting the heel of my hand to make whatever is happening stop. It doesn't.

The urge to bite deeper into my hand takes hold of me. It's all I want. It's all there is. I try to open my jaws but I can't. Maybe someone should spray me in the face with a water hose like they do to pit bulls that won't let go. The urge is so strong. I don't know if I can fight it anymore. What's wrong with me? God, I want to bite! My teeth are starting to break skin. Do it! Do it now! I want to sink my teeth in quick, before I can think about it anymore. I want to yank my head back and rip free a hunk of muscle and tissue.

I can see the blood in my mind and know how bad it would look. I can see the alarm on my co-worker's faces. I'd be taken to the ER. Holy crap! All the attention. All the shame. People looking at me. Questions I can't answer. Well-deserved judgment. A nightmare. With effort I unclench my teeth and lower my hand to the desk. The imprint of my teeth is deep and already looks to be bruising. I reach for the desk phone next to me and call Faith at work.

"Hey!" says my wife and I can hear the smile in her voice. "Good morning, Sweet."

"Hey," I say and already feel my blood pressure edge back down a few points. "How are you? How's your morning?"

"Ughh. You know. Busy again."

"Mmmm. Us too." I try to sound conversational but something in my tone must come through. Faith pauses.

"You okay?" she asks.

I sigh and my eyes dart around the room gauging the level of privacy that my little corner provides. At the moment, only the secretary is at the station and she is at the adjacent desk on the phone. I turn into the corner a little farther and lean against the wall next to me. "I don't know, Hon. There's something wrong with me, I think." I close my eyes, already embarrassed by my confession. "I'm kinda freaking out or something. My heart is pounding so hard."

Faith listens, waits for more. I don't know what else to

say. "Did you check your blood pressure? Maybe it's up," she suggests.

"I'm sure it is but that seems more like a symptom than a cause." She doesn't understand what I'm trying to say and I'm too embarrassed to elaborate. I try again. "I feel so nervous. It came on all at once. And…" She waits. "I want to bite my hand."

"What do you mean, you want to bite your hand?" she says, her voice is more careful now.

"You know, to make it stop. I want to bite it…hard." I know I'm being cryptic but what do I say? I feel so stupid. Thank God, we have been married long enough that being able to read each other's minds is a perfectly reasonable expectation. I wait for her to do this now. Please don't make me say more.

She inhales a long breath. "I think you may be having a panic attack." She keeps her voice calm, reassuring. "Have you ever had one before?"

I shake my head. Then remembering I am on the phone add, "No." A panic attack. Something about that hits home. It feels right. God, if this is what a panic attack feels like, I have new respect for people who say they get them. When patients described them to me, I always thought they were just being dramatic. I always had to resist snorting. Thought they were being babies.

I open my eyes, shift in my seat and scan the nurses' station again. Still empty. "What the hell causes a panic attack?" I say keeping my voice as low as I can. "I wasn't doing anything. When it came on, I mean. I was in a patient room just finishing an admission database on the computer. That's it."

"I don't know," Faith answers. "It might not have anything to do with what you were doing though."

"It was so sudden and so powerful that I had to leave the room." I rub my eyes with my other hand. "I just feel like I'm coming out of my skin. Or like I need to. Like I need to claw my way out of myself. Does that make any sense?" I ask knowing that it doesn't.

"Do you think you need to go to the ER? They could get you some medicine."

"God no," I say emphatically. "For a panic attack? They'd laugh me out of there. I have to work with these people." I heave a sigh. "Okay, I'd better go. I'm gonna go to the break room and get some hot milk. Maybe it will calm me down."

"Okay. Call me later. I'm worried about you," she says and I can tell she is.

"I'll be fine. If this is just a panic attack, it'll go away. I feel like such an idiot." I shake my head. "It's so intense though. No wonder people think it's something else. It feels like you're dying, or going crazy." Neither of us says anything for a minute. "All right. I gotta go. I'll call you later."

"Okay. I love you."

"Love you too," I say and hang up the phone. Oh man. Am I losing it or what? I take several slow breaths to try and slow my still-racing heart then head for the break room. Hot milk will help. Just wrapping my hands around the warm cup and feeling the rising steam on my face will do wonders for me. A panic attack. I can hardly believe it. This is nuts, I think to myself and notice for the first time that my hand is really beginning to hurt.

I do not have another panic attack, at least I do not have one right away. The anxiety remains with me as it has for weeks, a grating white noise constantly buzzing in the background of my mind. I do whatever I can to escape it.

I read when I can, less for pleasure now than for simple necessity. I need to escape, to get away from myself. I don't want to make decisions anymore, not even the small ones. I want to be a character in a book, anyone but me. Reading lets me become someone whose life has already been created and planned to exacting detail. All the decisions have been made by the author. I don't have to think. I just have to trundle along like a trolley on its tracks heading for my ultimate happy ending where everything will tie up neat as a Christmas package. My concentration is getting sketchy as is my ability to read for any length of time. Escape is becoming more elusive. When it is gone the real trouble begins.

Without reading my mind turns against me. It becomes the hated commentator pointing out the negative side of every aspect of life and of all of them, I am the worst. I have no drive it tells me, no personality, still and always a misfit. If my Censor just moped about, it might be tolerable but it doesn't. It obsesses without end. On and on it goes driving home the gravity of these issues. How awful I am. How crazy I am. How undeserving I am. Of course how I have made a mess of my life and am an embarrassment. It is relentless…and it is right.

I am bad. I am lazy. I am old. My best years are behind me. All that's left in life is mounting failure, poor health, and bone-weary exhaustion. I am ruining my daughter's life. I am ruining my wife's life. Everyone would be better off without me. It goes on from the time I wake each hateful morning till the time I sleep each night. I'm too worn down to ignore it. I no longer even try.

Sometimes violent and self-destructive thoughts come into my mind. The thoughts feel like they come from outside me, like they are being pushed into my head. The ideas are so compelling that I don't know if I can resist them. I don't want to die as much as I want to hurt myself. I want to do something horrible, something savage that cannot be undone.

I have to leave the kitchen when chopping vegetables because the urge to cut off my fingers is so powerful. I stand over the kitchen sink running the garbage disposal staring down into its clattering black mouth, fighting to keep from shoving my hand down it. I am hypnotized by the glowing heating element of the stove on high. I want to mash my hand down onto it and hold it there. I want to burn clear through my skin and right down to the bone. Maybe farther.

The thoughts of committing such horrific acts of violence against myself are confusing and extremely disquieting. They thrill me almost to the point of sexual arousal. It's why I'm so close to giving in to them. This, I realize, is just plain fucking crazy. What's wrong with me? How has my mind come off its tracks to such an extreme extent? I'm past caring if I live or die but I don't want to be tortured or disfigured. So where are these thoughts coming from? I have to shut them out before something happens but they're only getting worse.

Longing for stillness and quiet, I return to the 19th century and my sparsely furnished English flat that seems forever trapped in a winter's night. I have not come here since I was young. I am thrilled to find it just the way I left it. What's more, it seems that in moving backward in time, I briefly give my mind's anxieties the slip. They lie somewhere in the distant future. The flat remains as it always did, a temporary shelter where I can harbor for a while but no more. I am always drawn back, too soon, like a trout on a hook, to the press and urgency of my life in the present.

My agitation is intense and unremitting. It is surely obvious by this point. I have difficulty following anything people tell me and have no desire to do so anyway. Why can't people understand I don't want to talk to them? Speaking, like everything else, has become a loathsome and dreaded chore. Carrying a conversation is no longer within my skill set. I rub my face and wring my hands. I tuck myself into the corners of the bed, when I'm able. I do my best to become completely invisible.

# Chapter 25

# Deterioration

It is afternoon. I have left work and have driven by my stepdaughter's school to pick her up only to discover she has gone home with a friend. It's just as well. I'm in no shape to be responsible for another human being right now. I can barely look after myself. I pull out of the school parking lot and turn my car toward home. As I coast to a stop at the corner traffic light my mind drifts to today's latest failure at work. I have been called into my boss's office at least once a week for the past month to be counseled for one mistake after another. Today it was for leaving the hospital after my shift yesterday without giving a report on one of my patients to the oncoming nurse. My boss is exasperated. She told me that she doesn't understand what's wrong with me. What could I tell her?

Sitting at the intersection now waiting for the light to change, I am disgusted with my carelessness, disgusted with myself. I am certain I am going to lose my job if this continues. My boss likes me for some unknowable reason though.

It's probably the only thing that has protected me this long. My mistakes have not been small.

A car pulls up to the light on my right. There is one empty lane between us so I have a full and unobstructed view of it. I look at it sort of mindlessly and then frown as something beneath the front of the car catches my eye. To my horror, a thin sinewy arm, charred black from the intense heat, reaches down from the engine compartment. It uncurls its four long alien fingers and brushes them lightly against the road beneath the car. It is sinister and terrible and the sight of it fills me with dread. I look wildly to the woman behind the wheel. She is watching the traffic light, unaware of the danger she is in. In a panic, I think of honking and pointing but she might get out of the car to investigate. My God, this isn't happening!

Before I have any more time to think, the light changes and the woman accelerates into the intersection. Whatever is hiding in her engine compartment draws its arm back up and out of sight. Blinking against the shock of what I have just seen, I regain enough composure to accelerate along with her. The woman goes straight. I turn left. Just like that she is gone and so is my opportunity to warn her.

My heart is beating loudly in my chest. I drive the remaining blocks to my house stunned. A small rational voice somewhere in my head is telling me that I couldn't have seen what I thought I saw. It tells me to calm down, to think it through. I can scarcely hear the little voice, but a much louder voice is shouting at me to admit what very clearly was an interdimensional creature invisible to everyone else but me!

There must be an entire race of these things living amongst us unseen. The small voice suggests that perhaps my mind is slipping. Is it possible that maybe I am beginning to hallucinate? Okay, I am depressed, I concede. But what is WAY more likely, the big voice booms authoritatively, is that the altered chemistry in my depressed brain is precisely what allowed me to see the creature in the first place. I am the only one who knows what's going on!

And here, the big voice begins, softer now that it has my complete attention, is the really scary part. I wasn't supposed to see it. I know this intuitively to be true. And it knows that I saw it! The irony then, I realize with chilling certainty, is that the woman in the car was safe all along. The one in danger, was me...is me.

By the time I pull into my driveway at home, I understand. I understand that I will now be hunted and threatened by an invisible race of interdimensional creatures that may or may not try to kill me because I saw one of them and from that sighting, gleaned their existence. What I fail to understand at this point, however, is that I am as crazy as a shit house rat.

When I get out of the car, I step quickly away from it leaving the door wide open. The hair stands up on the back of my neck. I stare at it in something close to terror. Slowly and from what I judge to be a safe distance, I squat down and lower the side of my head to the cement in order to get a good view of the underside of my car. Nothing. No creature. I breathe a little easier. But only a little. I will have to be on my guard now. My life depends on it. There's no way to unsee what I have seen. There's no going back. I kick the door closed with my foot.

In the weeks that follow this incident, I am on high alert. I cannot stop thinking about the creatures. I have difficulty sleeping, afraid that they will kill me when I am unconscious. They are everywhere. In the shadows, in my house, at the hospital. They are following me. They want me to know they are there. They are watching me, seeing if I will tell anyone about them. If I do, I know they will kill me.

There is a green car that I see all over the place near my home. It is connected to the creatures in some way. I know this from the cold fear I feel when I see the car, like icy claws squeezing my heart. I am attuned to them now. I feel them when they are near. I don't know if they are reminding me with the car that they are watching or if it is simply a vehicle they use to conduct their business. Maybe it is driven by a human that is allied with them or is being forced to do their bidding. If I see the car while driving, I immediately turn off and try to get away from it. If it drives by on the street outside of my house, I snap the shutters closed and wait until I know it is gone.

During this time I am somehow still functioning. Not well, mind you, but I do not miss a single day of work. My days are black and agitated, filled with paranoia and confusion. I am miserable in ways I never knew I could be. Pacing helps or going on long walks. The repetitiveness of the movement soothes my sandpaper thoughts.

One rainy afternoon while on one of these walks, I

consider that death by walking would be a wonderful hypnotic way to die. It is only mid-March and so far this year, still cold. If I were to walk north and just not stop, I would eventually die. This is really good.

I would carry no identification. I would drink no water, eat no food, and never stop to sleep. I would walk for days, maybe a week, until I collapsed from exhaustion and dehydration. No one would know where I was. I would lose consciousness and die from exposure just out of sight from the interstate. My body would go unclaimed. It is a comforting thought but I don't do it. Instead I return after my walk to take care of my kids. As always, responsibility and obligation win out and I go on breathing another day.

In May, the kids get out of school for the summer. My stepson is graduating from high school this year. Technically, he already has but his class has yet to stage their graduation ceremony. It is Saturday afternoon and Faith's family wants to have a celebratory dinner for him to acknowledge his accomplishment. We are trying to get dressed and ready to meet them at a local restaurant. It is now that I have the second panic attack of my life. I have no reason to have it, but this one is even worse than the last time when I was at work and wanted to bite a chunk out of my hand.

This time I feel it coming on but there is nothing I can do to stop it. Oh God, I'm coming apart again. What on earth is wrong with me? I hate myself. I hate my guts. I'm such a fucking freak. I struggle against it but it takes me anyway.

I am mumbling and ranting nonsense. My heart rate is skyrocketing. Faith has no more idea what has happened than I do. I begin marching around the room. I have lost all control. Finally I just state, "There is no way that I can go to dinner like this. You deserve better than me. I'm no good for you." Then I run out the front door of the house.

I have no idea what I am doing. I only know I have to run or I will explode. I keep running until I can't run anymore. I'm no longer 17. I make it no more than a few miles from home before heat and exhaustion and age bring me to an inelegant stop. I am drenched in sweat and my breathing is ragged.

My thoughts are still a little wild but I have control of myself again. I look around and try to figure out where I am. Taking stock of my situation I conclude that I am miles from home, with no car, no cell phone, no wallet, and no house keys. Nice. With no other options open to me that I can think of, I begin to walk home.

Faith is, of course, gone by the time I get there. This as much as anything tells me she is getting frustrated with my behavior. I feel terrible. I am an awful husband and stepfather. Everyone is at the restaurant. I know I should be there too to support my stepson. What is he thinking of me? What had gone wrong? I was okay one minute and the next I couldn't breathe. I couldn't think. I was in a blind panic.

"Wait. Panic! That's it. Shit! Are you kidding me? Did I just have another panic attack?" I am shouting out loud to myself in the house and gesturing with my arms. I run upstairs and pass through the shower. I dress in a rush and drive, like the madman that I am, to the restaurant to meet my family. Better late than never.

When I arrive, everyone is happy to see me but something about my appearance seems to be cause for alarm. Conversation trails off and one by one they all turn to look at me, concern on their faces. I'm fine. I'm fine, I tell them as they ask if I am all right. I begin to worry that I might have the look. The one that homeless guy has downtown who hangs around the bus station. Not quite right. Disturbed. People can see it. I try to ignore the thought.

My face is flushed and I am perspiring again so badly that my hair is pasted to my forehead and trickles of sweat are running down my face into my eyes. I swipe at them irritably, embarrassed. My shirt is nearly soaked through with sweat and sticking to my skin. Didn't I just put this on a little while ago?

I congratulate my stepson. Try to look normal. We hug and share a laugh. He is relieved that I am here. I take my seat and drink an entire pitcher of water. Faith leans over and quietly asks me, yet again, if I am okay. I nod and smile, avoid her eyes. It seems, though, I am not convincing. Not convincing at all.

Evening, not long after my second panic attack. I am home alone. My black and scattered thoughts swirl about me like dead leaves and garbage before a storm. I light a candle. When it has caught, I blow out the match and the smell of burnt wood rises to my nostrils. A memory of peace and mental stillness comes back to me from long ago. In my right mind, the memory of burning myself would make me feel embarrassed even in the privacy of my own head. I would shake it out as quickly as I could. Now all I feel is the certainty that this will work.

I don't dwell on it. I don't think that I am about to cross some sort of invisible line. I just strike another match and watch the flame for a moment, absently, then blow it out and press the glowing match head to the skin inside of my forearm. There is no pain. I am blank.

I do it again, this time snuffing the flame out directly on my skin. This time there is pain but it's dull, distant. I wait. Then it drifts over me like a gentle breeze. I drop the spent match on the counter and close my eyes. My thoughts center. Quiet. Finally. I repeat the process twice more for good measure, then sweep the evidence from the counter into my palm and drop it in the trash.

Later the same week I do it again. There is no regret, no sensation of failure as I fall back into old habits, only weariness. I don't understand what's happening. I know depression well. It's never been like this though. I'm so edgy. I dispose of the matches when I am done; disappointed by the already fading relief they brought me.

By the following night, I am in need again. I am in the middle of cooking dinner. Faith is not home yet and the kids are with our exes. Normally I listen to music as I cook. Lately I can't bear music. Instead I listen to the unending negative monologue in my head, my lips moving as I mumble along with the words.

I consider the problem. The burns aren't t working. They only help for a few minutes and then the static is back, the agitation, the crawling, anxious, rotting from the inside. I am desperate. "Maybe I just need a bigger burn," I say out loud and fill a small pan with water. I put it on the stove and heat it to a roiling boil.

I consider pouring the scalding water over my arm but it seems too hard to control. Instead, I take a glass coffee cup from the cabinet and fill it with the boiling water right from the stove, then I slide to the floor with my back against the dishwasher and the steaming mug in my hand. I hesitate for no more than a breath, then press the mug against the inside of my opposite forearm.

Okay, this hurts. In an odd way, this surprises me. I close my eyes. Wow. This hurts a lot. Still, I don't take the mug away. My plan was to hold it in place until the water cooled the way I do with the matches, but I don't know how long that will take. I don't want to find out. After less than 10 seconds I have to pull it away. It leaves an angry, red, mug-sized burn on my skin.

I lay my head back against the dishwasher and wait for the pain to subside. It doesn't. There is the momentary sensation of peace but it is fleeting, no more effective than the matches. After a long minute, I sigh and heave myself to my feet. Feeling more hopeless than ever, I pour the water down the sink and watch the steam rises from the drain. So much for that.

Waking up the following morning, I am surprised to see that the burn on my arm is one enormous and very ugly fluid-filled blister. This is going to be impossible to hide. It looks really bad. I inspect it with mild annoyance. So not worth it. Now I remember the flaw in trying to burn the awful out of me…unwanted attention.

At work I lance the wound, drain the fluid, and cover it with a dressing. I tell anyone who asks that I burned it on a pan while cooking dinner. It's almost the truth. I was cooking dinner. The lie satisfies my co-workers but Faith is not so easily fooled. She has been watching my steady descent these past few months and is not taken in by the ole "burned it on a pan while cooking dinner" yarn. She knows exactly what it is and how it got there. Early on, she suggested I go and see a doctor, get back on some medication. Later she begged me. Now she won't take no for an answer and this time, finally, I give in.

# Chapter 26

# Hanging My Head

The earliest I can get in to see a psychiatrist is two weeks away, but that's not bad in the world of mental health care. By the time I make it to the appointment I am pretty much a wreck. I sit in the waiting area fidgeting and wringing my hands non-stop. When they call me to the back, I meet the Psychiatric Nurse Practitioner, or NP, who will be managing my care. She shows me to her office and directs me to sit. The attending psychiatrist pops his head in to introduce himself then disappears somewhere to bill my insurance for it. I will never see him again.

Perched rigid on the edge of the chair, I am coiled and ready to spring to my feet at the first sign of trouble. I want to run, or shout, or clear everything off the NP's desk with a broad swipe of my forearm. There is so much potential energy in my posture that it snaps off me like electricity. I charge the entire room with crazy.

I stand up and pace back and forth in front of the window then sit back down. I repeat this several times throughout the hour-long initial appointment. The interdimensional beings are near. I can feel them warning me, monitoring everything I say. Their message is clear. I am not to speak of them. I wouldn't dare. We have an uneasy truce and I won't jeopardize it. Telling anyone would serve no purpose and only put us all in danger. It is my responsibility to remain silent on this point in order to protect myself and those around me.

The NP runs down a list of questions she has on the laptop in front of her. She doesn't want any elaboration. She wants a quick answer in as few words as possible since whatever those words are, she will have to type into the program.

The questions are generic like they came from an "Are You a Nutcase? Take the Quiz" article in the back of a magazine. I wonder when we get to the end of the program if it will generate a diagnosis based on my responses and send an appropriate prescription to the printer for me to pick up when I check out. Maybe this doctor could just put some self-service kiosks in the waiting area for all of us patients to use and save himself the trouble of hiring a NP at all.

Whatever. I just want some relief. I can't live like this anymore. When the NP gets to the question about whether I have ever seen a psychiatrist before, I answer yes. This generates another series of questions which I'm sure annoys her to no end. For what? What was the outcome? Was I given a diagnosis? For the first time in my life, I don't bother trying to deny it or hide it. I look out the window to my left. The sun is shining, the Texas sky broad and cloudless.

"Bipolar," I say without emotion and the NP glances at

me over the top of her glasses.

I answer honestly all the questions the NP asks me. The only thing I omit, thereby saving both of our lives, is the fact that there are interdimensional beings hiding in people's engine compartments and I am the only one who knows they exist. Throughout the interview it is impossible for me to sit still. I jiggle my leg. I wring my hands. I rub the sides of my face and my eyes. I pace. When we are finished, I find out at last what is wrong with me.

There is, it seems, a curious phenomenon known as a mixed state. It is one of the more unpleasant dishes served from the bipolar menu of episodes. In a mixed state, also known as dysphoric mania or agitated depression, symptoms of both mania and depression exist at the same time. The NP tells me that most patients say that this convergence of symptoms feels much worse than either depression or mania alone.

Often present in mixed states are feelings of hopelessness, agitation, and racing thoughts usually dark or morbid in nature such as self-hatred, worry or guilt. Also common are impulsivity, panic attacks, and rage. Some people experience psychosis, paranoid delusions, compulsions to self-harm, and suicidal thoughts. In fact, statistics show that most bipolar suicides are carried out by people in a mixed state. A very nasty business indeed.

When I leave the office, I am carrying a fistful of prescriptions and an appointment card to be seen in again in a week. I fill the prescriptions on the way home and take the first dose as soon as I walk in the house and can get to a glass of water. Considering my past attitude toward psychiatric medication, this speaks as much as anything to my current level of desperation.

The meds sort of gork me out but they do their job. Within a month the mixed state has broken. Within two months I feel like myself again. Within five months, I toss out the meds and strike back out on my own. Why take medication for a fluke episode that will never occur again? I'm not some pale whiny kid from *The Secret Garden*. I'm sure the NP never even realizes I'm gone.

# Chapter 27

# Construction Frenzy

More than a year has passed without incident and I am feeling well. Once again I have changed jobs but am content in my new position. A depression is gathering strength like a hurricane far out in the Gulf but it won't make land for months. Right now I have no worries. The skies are clear today and it's easy to believe they'll stay that way forever. Besides the dry wilting heat of summer is behind me for the year and there is just something about the fall. It's so full of promise. I am always getting swept up in something like a fallen leaf on a cool breeze. This year it is boat building that lifts me with a whoosh high into the autumn sky.

My mood, as it often does, begins to lift with subtle but noticeable effect beginning around September. I find myself laughing more and becoming more sociable at work both with my patients and my co-workers. I tell jokes and stories. I take an interest in the tiniest details of other people's lives. I enjoy my job and family. And my mind begins to wake up.

Some years ago I lived in a house with a Texas sage bush planted in the flower bed next to my front porch. It used to bloom every fall after the droughts of summer had passed and the rains had returned. Bright purple flowers would begin blooming all over it like starbursts, more and more each day until it was covered. I always found it odd that when the rest of the trees were beginning to gear down for the coming of winter, that bush seemed to be more alive than at any other time of the year. Is it any surprise that one was my favorite?

It is not unusual during the fall for ideas to start appearing in my mind like the flowers on that old sage bush. More and more every day until they fill my head. Often at these times, I begin carrying one of those marbled composition notebooks around with me to write down the ideas as they come to me. If I don't, they will get lost and buried under more ideas or forgotten like faded dreams. Many of them are good. Many more are stupid but all of them seem brilliant when they come to me.

This year I decide that I want to build my own wooden sailboat in my backyard. I will test it first in the lakes of North Texas and then in the Gulf of Mexico. If it passes its sea trials, I will provision it and sail it solo across the Atlantic. This obviously makes perfect sense.

For a couple of weeks I turn the details of my developing plan over and over in my mind with feverish intensity. It is important, however, that I do the leg work on this before I begin in earnest. I research research research boat building, sailing, seamanship, survival at sea, navigation by the stars, radios, GPS, autopilot rigs, etc. I review weather patterns across the Atlantic to determine the best routes and time of the year to make the trip. I read, and question, and send off about a million Google searches. I make lists and I try to figure out what to do about my hassling job.

About two weeks into this, the part of my brain that roots out foolishness and bullshit, at least when it has enough on the ball to recognize it as such, begins to consider my newfound obsession with a more suspect eye. I realize this could all be a waste of time. It would not be the first time that my episodic passions have caused me to pursue outlandish goals that I have no prayer of ever achieving. I'm aware that I do this sort of thing. All my plans might just turn out to be, well…stupid. It's why I don't go around anymore shooting off my mouth with all the details of my idiotic schemes.

So okay, maybe something smells a little off about my plan for a solo transatlantic voyage on a homemade boat, but as always, I have no interest in listening to anything negative that someone has to say on the subject, even if that someone is me. I am a visionary. Still, experience has taught me that my best chance for success in these ventures is often to allow the sensible part in me and the visionary in me to strike a compromise, to find some sort of reasonable middle ground that will satisfy everyone. It doesn't take long.

The visionary grants that sailing solo across the Atlantic is, for me, probably unrealistic. In fact, building a sailboat of any real quality is also, if I'm honest with myself, a fool's errand. The sensible part of me, on the other hand, grants that the visionary needs an outlet or project into which I can channel my boundless enthusiasm. The answer, the two soon agree, is a smaller boat!

During the preceding summer, I bought a three-man inflatable raft to play on with the kids in the creeks and waterways near our house. At the time, I kidded around about fitting it with a sail. Now the idea returns to me as an answer to my racing mind's dilemma. Sure it's stupid, but it's also harmless and definitely within my grasp. This is insight, baby. They don't come any saner than me!

From the beginning, I love everything about this idea. It will not draw unwanted attention or eye rolling. I won't have to hold my tongue or keep it a secret. People will just think it's whimsical not crazy. If it doesn't work, I'll be out very little money. I don't have to quit my job. And if I pull it off it will be a load of fun to take out on the lake and sail it around.

I've always wanted to teach my kids to sail but in North Texas it seems no place is willing to rent out even a cheap boat to anyone who hasn't completed a certification course which proves they know what they're doing. And unfortunately, anyone who has ever met me knows that I never have the slightest idea what I'm doing. No one can stop me if I build my own boat though. And the engineering challenge of turning an inflatable raft into a sailboat is exactly the sort of project that excites me.

My brain is starting to skip along at an ever faster pace and it feels exhilarating to give it some direction. I think of one idea after another, feeling supercharged as the boat takes shape in my mind. Each time I spot a potential problem my brain pounces on it like a kitten on a yarn ball and engineers a solution around it. Each one is like a puzzle and I chortle smugly at the cleverness of my solutions.

I'm a kid again and having the time of my life. I lay awake in bed at night forever tweaking and updating the boat's design. It's impossible to turn off the machinery in my head now that it is tasked with a job.

It becomes maddening to try and do my real job at the hospital when my thoughts are so completely engaged elsewhere. I fill the composition book, which I have started carrying again, with sketches, design notes, and supply lists. As soon as I believe that I have answered all the biggest questions posed by the design and construction…I begin.

My garage becomes my workshop and if I am not at work or at Home Depot buying more supplies, this is where I can be found. A better woodworker than myself could finish in a fraction of the time but I have no deadlines. The boat is taking shape and I'm having a ball.

The sail is my most significant challenge. If I only want to sail with the wind at my back pushing the boat, then I could run a bed sheet up the mast and it would work just fine. If, however, I want to be able to sail into the wind at even a shallow angle, which I do, then I will have to design and cut my sail to exacting specifications. Sail design is a science unto itself and these days relies on expensive computer software to make the calculations for cutting and sewing a sail with such specific performance capabilities.

The basic premise is that an efficient sail functions like a vertical wing. If cut and sewn correctly and the wind hits it, it will billow out into the shape of an airfoil. This shape gives the sail the ability pull to the boat upwind as well as push the boat downwind depending on how it is angled.

I am not intimidated by the complexity of this part of the project but rather eager for its challenge. People were making adequate sails long before computers, I reason, so I'm pretty sure I can handle it too. Once again I dive headlong into researching my topic. I scour the Internet, learning everything I can about sail performance and design. I buy an enormous book on the subject and add the expense without blinking to the already more than $500 tab I have so far run up.

I finish the sail and it looks amazing. With its completion, my boat is almost done. I mop up with the rigging and the rudder and then it's ready for the water.

A little spark of hypomania can give a person almost superhuman drive. It deludes you into believing that the only possible outcome for any project, once undertaken, is success. Time, cost, or other practicalities are mere trifles, effortlessly dodged like slalom flags as one races wild-eyed toward his or her goal. Many great books, inventions, or works of art have been created on the tireless shoulders of hypomania. And now, something completely stupid as well, a sailboat made out of an inflatable raft with a solid deck and transom that can seat two people in comfort, be assembled in a flash, and when disassembled, be carried inside of a Ford Fiesta. It's so stupid it just might be brilliant!

## Chapter 28

# Long Lost Judgment

Because the completion of the sail took longer than I expected, it is late November now and fall is fast becoming winter. The temperature of the air is brisk and the water is worse. Still the idea of waiting until spring to take the boat out on the water for a test sail is unthinkable. I am single minded in my determination to get my boat wet and safety is nothing more than an obstacle in my way so in yet another spectacular example of bad judgment, I leave waiting for better weather for the chumps.

The first Saturday after I have finished the boat that arrives with clear weather is launch day. The fact that it is windy as hell and the lake I choose for my maiden voyage is white capping is meaningless. Faith is visiting her mother a few miles away and has left me with the girls. My daughter and stepdaughter are both eager to accompany me and I see no reason to inform their mothers or anyone else of my plans. It quite simply never occurs to me. My tunnel vision, at this point, is complete. Cornelia, who is now 14, will be my first mate and Sadie, who is 12 and either too nervous or too wise to want to sail with us, will watch from the beach and film the event on her phone. The fact that the three of us and the boat, including its 9-foot mast all fit in my Fiesta is a victory in itself. So far, so good.

Facing the water, the wind is blowing hard from behind us out across the lake. I assemble the boat on one side of a cove that offers at least partial protection. The plan is to sail from one side of the cove across to the other and back again. We will be sailing straight across the wind parallel to the shore. Foolproof! The boat looks great, like it can't possibly fail. I am grinning with smug satisfaction. If I could, I would break a bottle of champagne across her bow but of course her bow is made of vinyl and inflated with air so, yeah.

Leaving our shoes on the beach, I push the boat into shallow water and Cornelia and I climb aboard. Our legs are already numbed to the knees by their brief exposure to the frigid water. I sit at the transom holding the tiller in one hand and the sheet line in the other. Cornelia sits forward near the mast manning the halyard. Our life preservers are stowed safely at home in the garage. Safety is for chumps. Winners don't need to plan for failure.

We both have ill-advised smiles pasted across our wind-blown faces. Thank God for kids too naive to talk us out of our stupidity. I relish the moment for a few seconds then give my first command as a skipper. Hoist the mainsail!

Cornelia pulls down on the halyard and my homemade sail shoots up the mast. We accelerate across the cove like a couple of Miami drug smugglers in a cigarette boat. It is way too windy to be sailing. A saner man would know this, or pretty much anyone with half an eye and half an ass. Cornelia and I laugh with glee as we rocket across the water. The smiling figure of Sadie on the beach with her phone held in an outstretched arm shrinks to a speck in an instant. The boat is performing like a dream, like I knew it would. Cornelia is laughing. I'm laughing. Who's the king of the world now, Jack? You ole son of a bitch! Then the rudder snaps off.

The boat turns sharply off the wind and loses speed. I whirl around to see the tattered remains of the rudder being dragged behind the boat. I roll onto my belly, out over the transom, and retrieve what's left of it. The stern of the boat digs in under my weight and icy water washes up over it soaking the front of my shirt. If I lie like this and hold the remains of the rudder under the water I am able to steer the boat just well enough to regain some control. The boat straightens, the sail snaps taut again, and we accelerate anew.

The wind is picking up. I know this is bad. The boat is critically damaged now and our control is spotty at best. Every second that goes by we streak farther away from where we put in. We need to get back right away. I call over my shoulder to Cornelia, "Get ready to come about!"

"What?" she calls back.

Right. It probably would have been better to spend a little more time on sailing instruction before we set out... or maybe I should just talk like a normal father and not a complete boob. "I'm going to turn the boat around. The boom is going to swing across from one side of the boat to the other. You have to duck so it doesn't hit you in the head as it passes over. Okay?"

"Okay."

"Ready?"

"Yeah."

Still laying on my belly and holding the rudder in my hands, I force it hard over amazed at how much wrist strength it takes at this speed. The boat turns on a dime. The boom swings across, missing Cornelia who ducks out of its path like a pro, water washes over the stern again soaking me a second time, and then we stall. Shit.

We are now facing more or less, in the right direction but the sail won't fill. Instead it flaps uselessly in the still strengthening wind. Without forward momentum, the rudder, what there is of it, is now useless. I can't control the direction of the boat. I tell Cornelia to pull in the angle of the sail but it refuses to fill. Pushing myself back into the boat, I sit up and try to position the sail myself. Frustrated, I can't understand why I am having so much difficulty. Then I get it.

Two things have changed since we got underway. First, the wind has changed, and second, thanks to the broken rudder, U-turning, and the stall, we have been blown a good ways farther out into the lake. From here, when we aim the boat back toward Sadie where we put in, that "point of sail" is actually facing slightly into the wind. The angle into the wind is not steep but I'm afraid it may be too much for my homemade sail. That is why it won't fill. Despite my research and careful calculations it seems that making a performance sail is trickier than I thought.

I call instructions to Cornelia over my shoulder while continuing to struggle with the rudder. I am trying to get her a more favorable angle to the wind and hoping to God the sail will fill again. Our efforts are in vain and the sickening weight of our predicament settles into my chest like a January flu. Just as fast as that, we are in trouble. How embarrassing.

The wind is relentless and growing stronger by the second. We are being blown sideways and the farther out we're pushed, the stronger the wind becomes. My design includes twin dagger boards that extend down into the water from the sides of the boat to function as a keel and prevent this sort of sideways slipping but the wind is too strong and our profile to it is too big. We are helpless. I give up on the rudder and sit up.

I yank down the sail to reduce our profile. I need a second to think. I look around, taking stock of our situation. It's worse than I thought. We've already been pushed clear out of the cove. We're now in open water and the wind is bullying us out even farther. Fuck. This is all happening too fast.

My mind shifts into that weird hyper mode like it does in moments just prior to accidents or disasters. It draws out time to a crawl and gives me that strange analytic clarity. In a heartbeat I grasp the weight of the unfolding events.

Since I can't sail back into the wind, I can't get us back to where Sadie is. One way or another, the three of us are about to get separated. And if I can't think of something fast, it's going to be by the width of this entire lake. Cornelia and I are going to be blown from one side to the other leaving Sadie alone on the beach. We will be on the north shore and she on the south.

Sadie has a phone but no real idea of where she is. It would be impossible for her to give anyone directions to come and get her. Cornelia and I have no phone so we couldn't help her. She would not realize we were in trouble, only see us sail away and disappear. When we didn't come back she would have to try and get help on her own. The police might even end up being called. Cornelia and I would wind up miles away on the other side of this vast lake, safe but with no way back. No. I have to keep us all together no matter what.

I consider all of my possible options and calculate their odds of success. They all suck but I identify the best of them anyway. Cornelia and I are closer to the far side of the cove, opposite from the side Sadie is on. Although we are out into open water, the lip of the cove on our side is formed by a peninsula that extends a bit farther out into the lake. It is not all that far away from where we are now. We can't sail to it but it might just be reachable if we swim for it right now. The word that makes me the most nervous is "might."

If I tell her to, Cornelia will jump for it. We could abandon the boat and swim for the peninsula. Who cares about the boat anyway? It's only a toy. I know she could make the swim with ease on a lazy summer afternoon. Like me, she's good in the water but it's not a lazy summer afternoon.

It's deep here, the lake is white capping, the temperature is dropping now that afternoon is moving toward evening, and although the sky remains clear the wind out here feels like a gale. We would have to swim against it all the way in freezing water. If the current and the wind are too strong for her…if the water is too cold…she could drown. Something like twenty people a year drown in this lake. And none of them thought it was possible until it happened to them.

It may be misplaced confidence but I'm pretty sure I can make it. I'm unwilling to risk Cornelia in the water, not if I can help it. At least if she's in the boat she'll be safe even if that means safe on the other side of the lake.

Making the swim on my own is unacceptable though. It would mean abandoning Cornelia. She'd be alone without a phone and terrified as she hurtled across the lake in the deteriorating conditions. Sadie and I could jump in the car and race around the lake but how would I find her again? No way. It doesn't matter who I stay with. If we split up we're all screwed. Again, the only acceptable option is to keep us somehow together.

That just leaves trying to swim the distance to the peninsula dragging the boat with Cornelia in it. I don't like the odds of success but they're only getting worse. My chances, such as they are, diminish a little more with every second I waste thinking about it. The fucking wind is bulldozing us right out to sea. The little peninsula, our last chance, is already beginning to look out of reach. If there's any chance at all of me making it, I have to go right now. It may already be too late.

Out of options and out of time, I turn to Cornelia. "I have to go in and I have to go now."

"Wait, what?" she says but I am already over the side.

The water is so cold it sucks the air from my lungs. I hook an arm over the front of the boat and begin side stroking like I'm swimming for Olympic gold. My legs are scissoring beneath the boat while my free arm reaches and pulls at the water with all my strength. I slow us first then manage to hold our position. We aren't losing any more ground but we aren't gaining any either, not against this wind. This is what I was afraid of.

I push my body harder. It's folly but what choice do I have? I know I'll only be able to pour out this kind of energy for a short burst, not near long enough to make the shore, but how else can I overcome the force of the wind? If I can at all.

I give it everything I have and then give it a bit more. There is no plan B. The specter of failure is near. I can't believe what is happening. I tell Cornelia to try and get a little more of the sail down and then lay flat in the boat. I want her to reduce our profile as much as she can. The wind is kicking our asses. My breathing is so labored she has difficulty understanding me. I heave and slash and claw at the water. I curse the fucking wind. I keep it up for as long as I can but then way too soon, my strength fails me.

My pace begins to falter. Cornelia's expression edges from concern to fear. I feel sick. I'm gasping for air. She trusted me. I've always been the one to save her. She's never seen me fail. What happens if I can't do this? What happens then?

I think back on the whole venture of the boat. I knew I was hypomanic. I knew my judgment had lost a few steps but none of it seemed to matter. Mania knows no consequences. Now I have put my kids at risk. I am disgusted with myself.

The cold and exhaustion begin to turn my muscles to stone. My brain is still sending the messages, still commanding my legs to kick harder but they're slowing down against my will. I begin to sink lower in the water. I know we're at a pivotal point. It was a gamble trying to drag the boat against this wind. I knew that. Still, admitting I've lost is painful. Do I now take a further gamble and call Cornelia into the water with me, or do I cut my losses, and keep her safe by telling her to stay with the boat while I try to go it alone?

Without the boat I think maybe I could still make it to shore. Cornelia is fresh. She could make it. We could dive down under the wind driven current near the surface. We could gain the ground I haven t been able to dragging this boat. But what if I'm wrong?

For a moment I look up and notice the sky. It is blue and cold, oblivious to the little drama playing out far beneath it. To it, Cornelia and I are less even than specks. I feel a little sorry for us both. Everything always works out until the day that it doesn't.

The white caps are breaking over my head now and I'm choking on the water. As my body continues to try and shut down, it occurs to me for the first time that I might be in danger of drowning myself. I realize, like when I was in the boat, it's now or never. My strength is almost gone. My head is slipping beneath the water. I crane my neck to keep a tiny oval of my face above the surface. Though I try to hang on, my arm is beginning to slip from the boat.

I gasp to Cornelia. "You—have—to—jump," one word per ragged breath. I wonder if this will be the decision that saves us or the worst decision in the long string of bad decisions that I made today…the one that ends in a real disaster. Being split apart would be bad but one of us being dead would be infinitely worse.

Cornelia's face appears over the bow. She sees I'm in trouble but can't quite believe it. I can tell she doesn't want to attempt this swim. She looks toward the peninsula and back at me.

"No, Daddy! Don't give up. You're doing it. We're almost there just a little more. You can do it."

I am filled with desperation and misery. She won't let me quit. She still believes in me.

"Come on, Daddy! Swim!" she says looking from me to the shore and back, pleading.

God, can't she see I'm finished? There's nothing left. She still thinks her dad is invincible like when she was a little girl. All I have to do is look into her eyes and tell her, I can't do it. All I have to do is let her down…but I can't. My lungs are burning. I'm slipping under the boat. Why can't she see this for what it is? That's when I give up.

I don't give up swimming. I just give up on the idea of trying to save us both. She's going to stay in the boat. Good. It's smarter. At least one of us has some sense. She's not going to drown and I'm relieved that I don't have to make any more decisions. I'll keep pulling as long as I can for her. I know that there is no hope left to make it but I don't know what else to do. I feel sad for my daughter. Despite her little girl's naive belief in me, we're going to be blown across this lake or I'm going to drown before her eyes and traumatize her. Either way, she's going to find out soon enough that it was too much for me. I just can't bring myself to tell her so. I'll die first.

There's barely a flicker of life left in my muscles but I commit to wasting what's left of it on the impossible task of pulling us through this wind. I don't bother keeping anything in reserve for myself for when this fails. If I'm right, I'm already past the point of no return anyway.

As it turns out, however, Cornelia was right. Although I couldn't t see it from my vantage point so low in the water, I have made progress, much more than I thought. And what's more, the natural slope of the land on the peninsula creates a slight wind break. From where we are now there is far less wind to fight, so even with my strength nearly gone and my stokes as weak as a baby's, we are still moving forward.

When in disbelief I realize this, my hope is rekindled. Is it possible we'll make it after all? I find some last vestige of energy that I didn't know was there and my lactic acid-filled muscles eke out a few more exhausted strokes. Then at long last, my feet touch the muddy bottom.

I walk the boat into the shallows breathing so hard I can't speak. Cornelia climbs out and helps me drag it onto the beach then I collapse to my hands and knees. Unsure of what else to say or do, Cornelia sits on the front of the boat and waits for me to recover. Neither of us says anything. The wind is still howling but I don't care. We're on land and we're all on the same side of the lake. We can walk back from here. Everything is going to be okay.

After what seems like forever, my breathing returns to normal. I stand up on shaky legs then look off down the beach. Sadie is in the distance walking toward us.

"Well," I say and turn to glare at my boat. "That really could have gone better."

Cornelia smiles. "Yeah."

# Chapter 29

# Arrival

The hypomania of the previous autumn burns itself out just before Christmas 2012 like a fire that runs out of fuel. The holidays pass and I am relieved to see them go. I drift into January with an ominous dropping of my mood barometer. The storm has arrived.

This depression doesn't waste time with a lot of threatening skies and rumbling thunder. It rolls right in with authority and takes me apart. The power lines that feed my ability to care about anything at all are cut so fast and so cleanly that I don't even realize what has happened. Everything just stops for me.

I lose my ambition, my dreams, my drive, my emotions, and my interest in self-preservation. I no longer have a profession, no family, no self, no loves, no likes, no hopes, and no chance. The only need I feel is the need to feel itself, the need to feel anything at all. But I can't. All that is left in the world are unending and unwelcome responsibilities to which I must attend. I am numb. I am dead flesh animated.

If I still possessed the ability to feel stunned by the suddenness of it all, I would.

After so much experience with it, I have an impressive tolerance for depression. When at last I realize what I'm experiencing is the return of another depression, I do not shrink from it. It is what it has always been, a distasteful but endurable part of my life. As long as I don't get the terrible agitation of that mixed episode a couple of years ago, I figure I can get through just about anything else. That made me nuts. Complete emptiness takes a surprising toll on a person.

Faking normalcy requires a commitment I can't make anymore. It requires a concern for others' opinions that I don't have anymore. I soon abandon anymore half-hearted attempts to appear what I no longer am and what I cannot even remember being. My life becomes all business. I complete my tasks and no more. My smile, my humor, my interest in anything going on around me, all are gone. I have heard people with a flat affect described as having the lights on but nobody home. I'm pretty sure that I don't even have the lights on.

My hope is that this depression doesn't have any legs. It will pass in a few weeks, maybe a month, but when a month becomes two, and it shows no signs of easing its grip, I begin to falter. My thoughts, the few that I am still able to generate, grow dark. Death and dying become my focus yet again. It seems to me that a bright future is nothing more than an illusion of youth. Optimism is nothing more than a synonym for naivety and hope is a lie I can no longer keep telling myself. My fatigue becomes total and all that remains is the urge to let go.

Suicide is a logistical nightmare. When one considers the details and ramifications it is easy to become overwhelmed and right now brushing my teeth overwhelms me. One of the many details that I hang up on is the whole mortal sin concept, the idea that in God's eyes, killing myself is unforgivable and punishable by an eternity in hell. I mean who wants that, right? And yet it seems so unfair. Is life a gift we can decline with a, "thank you anyway," or a punishment we have to see through to the end like a sentence in the Gulag?

I consider the legal system's "not guilty by reason of insanity" plea. If the Court can show leniency to a person who commits a crime while not in his right mind, should God himself be less understanding…less merciful? After all, isn't depression an illness that equates to a state of temporary insanity? Couldn't the act of committing suicide itself be proof that a person is not in their right mind?

Should those who release life because they can no longer endure their suffering, or as in my case can simply no longer feel anything and become too fatigued to continue, be dealt the harshest punishment possible? Is that an unpardonable crime that draws the same penalty as ax murdering a busload of orphans? Really? Is it?

I think of the people through the years who have died at their own hand. I wonder if they are resting in a black oblivion, are happy and at peace in heaven, or are they burning in hell for their choice. For some reason Virginia Woolf comes to mind.

There are a lot of ways to kill yourself and some are easier than others. To fill your pockets with rocks and walk out into a river to drown cannot be for sissies. A person who does that, I reason, must have moved beyond any and all hope. If I were God, I would give that person a pass, mortal sin or not. I would.

The night that this thought comes to me is a Friday night in early March. I am sitting alone in an Italian restaurant having a glass of wine and an appetizer. I asked Faith to come with me but she declined. She has been upset with me more and more lately. If I could be bothered to analyze it I might realize that it is probably because the depression has made me less and less available to her as a husband. I cannot be bothered though. To me it just feels like I cannot please her and this adds yet another drop in the bucket of my weariness.

My hope had been that the sounds and smells of a cozy restaurant at dinnertime, the clinking dishes, the quiet conversation of lovers, and the soft lighting along with a good cabernet might ease my increasing disassociation with life. It hasn't worked. The cabernet is not bad though.

When I am finished, I pay the check and walk to my car. The temperature is crisp, maybe 37 or 38 degrees. There are about a million stars visible in the clear night sky. I push my hands a little deeper into the pockets of my coat. In the car I put on the heat full blast and turn toward home.

The small interior of the car feels safe. It is dark and protective. I am hidden. The tiny lights of the dashboard and console give off a comforting glow like the night light in Cornelia's nursery when she was a baby.

I don't want to go home yet. I'm not ready to see the unwashed dishes in the sink, the unfolded laundry on the couch or the stack of bills on the table. Neither am I ready to see the wife who I cannot satisfy. All the reminders of things I must do and things I am failing to do well or at all.

I don't make the conscious decision to drive to the big pond in a nearby neighborhood not far from my home. I just drive until I stop and when I do, I am there. I park at the curb and look out over the black water. It is not inviting. Still I get out of the car and make my way down to its banks. It feels colder here close to the water than it did at the restaurant. I squat and dip in my fingers. The water is cold but only physically.

I am thinking of Virginia Woolf again, wondering if I could do what she did. I do not want to commit suicide, not tonight. I haven t made peace with the idea, haven't sorted out all the details or the implications. Not yet. I'm just wondering. Would it be hard or a sweet relief to take that first breath of icy water?

I used to think there were good and bad places to die. I'm not so sure anymore. One place seems as good as the next. Warm in your bed, surrounded by your family or alone underwater in the freezing darkness. Does it really matter?

I stand up. The neighborhood is quiet. No one carrying a sack of garbage to the curb. No one walking a dog. I can just make out the sounds of traffic coming from the highway about a mile off, the distant thrum of wheels on asphalt. There is the faint smell of mud and wet shore plants. I can see my breath.

I shrug out of my coat and drop it on the moist ground behind me. I'm still wearing my scrubs from work, short sleeved and thin as a pair of pajamas. I don't take off my shoes. Why bother? I look out across the flat inky water for a moment and then walk out into it.

My feet sink into the soft bottom as I go and the mud sucks at my shoes. When I am a little more than waist deep I stop. Somewhere far away it registers that the water is cold but only as a footnote that I ignore. It holds no practical interest for me. My skin is as numb as my mind. I swirl my hands beneath the surface and watch the ripples drift out across the pond. I take a breath, bend my knees and sink in over my head.

As soon as my head dips below the water the world goes silent. I lean forward, push off with my feet and glide out into the blackness. It is like I imagined it would be, peaceful, empty. In this moment there are no more responsibilities, no more expectations. No one knows I am here. They cannot see me or need me. It occurs to me that right now...I am almost gone.

I can hold my breath almost turtle-like and I am still lean enough that I do not bob to the surface when underwater. These qualities combine now to give me a long needed respite. I hang weightless in the dark and resist the temptation to inhale. I know it could all be over that quickly. In an odd way, what could be more fitting? It's always been water with me. I don't know why I'm drawn back to it again and again.

Thoughts of my family come to me. It is not love that I feel, nor compassion, nor sorrow. I will not miss them. It's not personal. I will not miss anyone. I will not miss anything. The part of me that feels tenderness and affection has stopped functioning along with everything else. Almost everything. They say that when a person dies, hearing is the last of the physical senses to go. The last sentiment to go, however, may well be duty.

I cannot leave my family. Not now. I cannot abandon them to clean up the mess I would leave behind. The loss of my income alone would devastate them. The impact of my death could derail my kids' college and career plans. I have heard that family members of people who have committed suicide endure a unique and terrible kind of suffering. It could change everything for them. I didn't even leave a note. No. I took on this responsibility and it cannot be untaken. I have to see it through.

I hang suspended for another precious minute, then stroke once and drift back toward the world that waits for me. When my head breaks the surface the sounds of the night return. I wipe the water from my eyes and look back at the shore knowing what it represents and what is waiting for me there. I sigh and begin to breast stroke reluctantly toward it. After a couple of pulls, I am able to stand again and can walk the rest of the way in.

I climb onto the shore almost losing a shoe again to the mud. I am wearing running shoes but you'd never know it. They could be wooden clogs from Holland under all that mud. I will have to wash them when I get home. Another chore. Another "thing to be done." For the first time since I arrived here I feel cold. I pull my coat on over my dripping scrubs and trudge the short distance back to the car reclaiming the items of my unwanted life. Once inside, I turn the heat on high again but it doesn't help. By now I am shivering hard and cannot stop. I'm so cold. Still, it's comforting in a way. Maybe there are things I can still feel after all.

# Chapter 30

# Meeting the Man

That night I dream I am on a roller coaster. I am gripping the lap bar as tight as I can. I am not scared but it is not fun either. It is just something I am enduring. It feels like I have been on it a really long time.

I go careening down a near vertical drop and feel my stomach come up into my throat. At the bottom, the car pulls out of its death dive and shoots over a smaller hill. I can see at the bottom to this hill that the track will take the cars into a sort of tunnel.

There is a large wooden beam above the opening to the tunnel. From this angle it looks like I will crash right into it but I know this is an illusion. I have ridden on these things before. At what seems like the last minute I will dip under the beam and clear it by a mile. I will rocket safely into the tunnel and out the other side...only this time I don't.

With the momentum from the big hill pushing me, I fly over the smaller hill like a runaway locomotive. By the time it registers to me that there is not enough clearance under the crossbeam, it is too late. I never even have time to duck.

There is a sudden bang and the dim knowledge that something unyielding has hit me in the forehead with great force. My head is snapped back so hard I wonder if I have been decapitated yet there is no pain. There is no sound either. The instant I hit the crossbeam all of my surroundings disappear. It is quiet.

I don't understand. I am just standing somewhere. Nothing about the place is familiar. I feel fine but have no idea where I am or how it is that I have come to be here. Then I see the man.

He strolls up to me with the hint of a grin on his lips and a twinkle in his eyes. Maybe he has come to help. It's probably obvious that I am lost. He seems relaxed like he knows where we are so I ask him.

"Say, uh...I thought I was just on a...well, a..." I hesitate realizing how odd it's going to sound when I say it aloud. I thumb back behind me in a vague gesture and furrow my brow. I am unsure of how to continue.

"A roller coaster?" he finishes for me and smiles.

I stare at him in surprise. I open my mouth to say something but nothing comes out so I close it again. I blow out some air and settle for a nod. Then with a little determination I manage to add, "How did you...?"

He chuckles. It's a warm friendly chuckle and I can't help but smile back at him. He looks like he has good news, like he's Ed McMahon or something, standing on my front porch with and enormous cardboard check from Publishers Clearing House.

"You're done," he says as if that explains everything.

Somehow though, it does. I know exactly what he is referring to. Life. I look at him skeptically, afraid to hope. "Done?" I repeat.

He is beaming, watching my expression. "Done. Done," he says with finality.

Now a smile begins to creep across my lips too. I can't help it. Can this really be? If it is, it's better than any old sweepstakes check. I feel a laugh begin to bubble up all the way from my toes but I'm not quite ready yet to set it free. Is it possible to jinx dying? I raise my eyebrows at him tentatively.

Still smiling, he raises his own eyebrows and nods in response. My reserve breaks. I don't know how but I know he is telling me the truth and I start to laugh with relief and happiness. The man laughs with me. We laugh there together and I think that if letting people know they have moved beyond the trials of living is his job, then he must have the greatest job in the universe.

The initial giddiness begins to ebb. I regain control of myself and wipe away a stray tear from my cheek. It is a tear of happiness. It seems like forever since I have laughed this way. I let out a long contented sigh.

"I thought I was going to have to keep going like another forty years or something," I say to the man.

"Not you," he says. "You're done. This was your last day. It is, as they say, official."

I reach up and interlace my fingers behind my head. My face feels warm. I have no aches or pains. I think I should know this man but have yet to place him. It's like we are old friends. A question though comes to mind now. I am about to ask it when I stop. Maybe I don't want to know.

The man smiles at me as if reading my mind. "You did real good," he says.

Another short burst of laughter escapes from my chest. "Really?"

He nods, gives me a couple of seconds more to process things, then spreads his hands. "You ready?"

I know he is asking me to go with him. There is nothing I would rather do but then I remember my family. How could I have forgotten about them? What kind of father am I? What kind of husband? I don't move. "What about... them?" I say turning my head and nodding back behind me where it seems that life is.

He knows who I am talking about. Of course he does. I feel an immense love coming from him. He looks at me with such understanding and seems happy to answer any questions that I have. He puts a hand on my shoulder and says simply, "They're going to be just fine."

He is so certain. "Are you sure?" I ask.

Now it's his turn to let go a laugh. His eyes dance with delight at my question. "Trust me," he says.

I do too. I don't know why yet, but I do. Suddenly I feel a little silly for even asking but there is no judgment in his response. There is no judgment in this man at all.

"This is part of their journey," he says and I understand.

It's like when my own mother died. It shaped me in important ways. Every experience in life is important, even the bad ones. It makes us who we are.

Nothing is going to happen to them. Nothing can. They don't know that now but one day they will...again. One day they will stand where I am standing. One day they will meet the man.

The last of my earthly worries falls away and I am filled with the most profound peace I have ever known. I look at the man and smile. It is a goofy child-like smile. I make a dramatic sweep with my arm. "In that case," I say. "Lead on."

The man turns and begins to walk and I fall into step beside him. There is a beautiful light out in front of us and soon it is everywhere. I am not concerned. I do not look back.

When I wake Saturday morning I am heartbroken to find myself still living. I can remember the dream in vivid detail and it makes the years ahead of me seem even more insurmountable than they did the night before. I wonder if death will be like it was in my dream and how many more loathsome decades I will have to drag myself through before I can meet the man again. I wonder if there is a man at all. Did my mind just come up with him from a compilation of books and movies? Or was I just granted a peek?

## Chapter 31

# Futility

This depression has a stamina I have not yet experienced. Before I know it, it has swallowed five months of my life and shows no sign of easing its grip. I had hoped that the return of spring and then summer would bring back my spark but I remain where I am, stuck. I am somewhere between alive and dead, but neither truly one nor the other.

My ability to complete tasks has been reduced to only the most basic, those that must be done. No frills at this point, and no projects. My personality has vanished entirely. I speak to no one unless it is out of absolute necessity. Conversation is worse than torture. Thank God no one is trying to start them with me anymore. They can see there is something the matter with me and everyone is giving me a wide berth.

At last I decide I cannot live this way anymore, waiting for something to change. It is time to call a doctor. I have failed yet again.

Up until now, the difficulty in finding help has always been coming to terms with the idea that I do in fact need it. Once that bridge has been crossed the rest happens with relative ease. Now, however, I get my first taste of what so many others with mental illness go through trying to seek help.

My advice to any medical students who are as of yet undecided on a specialty would be to consider psychiatry. The mentally ill in our communities are woefully underserved and one problem you will not encounter is a shortage of patients. We're out here in abundance.

As I work at a large university hospital, my health benefits are pretty good. The only stipulation is that if I want to take advantage of their amazing rates I must see the doctors where I work. Outside of our system, however, the insurance coverage falls to that of most other companies, which is expensive as hell.

For this reason, I first seek out help in my own hospital's psychiatric clinic. There I am told that none of the doctors in the clinic are accepting new patients. None. I wonder what happens to the mentally ill patients who come in to the emergency room in crisis.

I let a week or so go by before I try again. This time I look at psychiatrists outside of my hospital system, those within ten miles of my home. I decide that things are becoming somewhat of an emergency and I am willing to pay a higher fee just to get some relief. I call no less than ten offices and receive the same response at each of them. No one is accepting new patients. Wow.

I call my own hospital clinic back and explain my dilemma. I emphasize that I am an employee and hope they make some exceptions for that. They don't. I am told, however, that I might be eligible for a depression study going on in the clinic and would be able to receive treatment free of any charge. Now we're getting somewhere.

After an extensive phone interview, which I pass, I wait a week for an interview with one of the researchers. At their office I fill out a pile of paperwork and answer countless more questions. In addition, I have to grit my teeth through a 45-minute long interview where I reluctantly confess the details of my mental health history. In the end I am told that because my depression is bipolar and not unipolar depression I am ineligible for the study. Oh for fuck's sake. Come on!

I am exhausted and frustrated. How was that not caught in the first phone interview? I'm sure they asked at that time and I'm sure I told them that I was bipolar. They tell me about another upcoming study on bipolar disorder that I could look into and hand me a business card with a number to call. It feels like it weighs about a hundred pounds.

So I'm supposed to go through the whole thing again from the start. Obviously, the people conducting the research are unaware of how much effort it takes a depressed person to make even a single phone call, fill out even the briefest of forms, or answer even the most mundane questions. If I could jump through this many hoops I wouldn't need help in the first place.

I just can't face repeating this same process a second

time for no more than the possibility of inclusion in another study. I decide instead to take another break and see if the depression will go away on its own. I mean how long can one of these things really last? I've heard stories of depressions that last a year or two, but that has never been my experience. I've got to be near the end. It has to break soon. Doesn't it?

# Chapter 32

# A Voice from the Past

All I want to do is sleep these days. Being unconscious is the only respite from living that really helps. If I am able to sleep, I sleep. If I can't sleep but have no tasks that I can't put off until later, I lie in bed anyway. As long as I don't have to face anyone or anything.

One Sunday morning I am lying in bed. It is around 11:30. I have been awake for hours but cannot drag myself out of bed to go to the grocery store. Still, I know this week's groceries aren't going to buy themselves any more than last week's clothes are going to launder themselves. I cannot remain in bed forever.

I am thinking at the moment, not of death but of life. I am thinking of the patients that I take care of and wondering what makes them cling so desperately to it. Why they are willing to subject themselves to almost any indignity for just a little more time in this world? What am I not seeing? Why am I so tired of it? What is broken inside of me that I would reject what they fight so hard for?

To the doctors, nurses and family members of the sick, death is a tragedy. Is it though? Why can't I feel that anymore? Why have I lost my connection to living, and how long will it take my body to release what my mind did months ago? I am tiresome to everyone around me. I know that. They all wish I would just snap out of it. That, or go on and die and be done with it so that they could move on. It's obvious on their faces when they are forced to be around me.

It's then that I hear her voice.

"Soon." She drags the word out in a soothing whisper.

I snap my head to the side to see who is crouching next to my bed but there is no one. I am alone. There is something about the voice though. I know this voice…and I know what she is talking about. It's my death.

She is breaking a rule. I am not supposed to know about my death but she is excited and can't wait. She wants to tell me. She is eager too, like me. I know her. My pulse quickens. Soon. Am I going home soon?

"When?" I whisper back. "Tell me when."

No answer. I can feel her though. She's still here. How do I know this woman? It's intimate, I feel certain. I search my deepest memories for her. Nothing. Wait. Lovers? Yes, lovers, I think. We were lovers. Before. Another life. Then it's gone. The memory darts away again before I can get hold of it like a silvery fish twinkling in the shallows. I try again. Got it. Not life…lives. It's why she is eager to reunite. She has missed me.

"When?" I say again. This time I am smiling. I can feel she is smiling too. She knows I have placed her voice. The air is electric around us. I can trust her. She will tell me the truth. I am straining to hear her again.

"October," she finally says and just like that, is gone leaving a vacuum behind her.

The news could not be better unless of course she had told me, next week. Nevertheless, my stay here on earth is almost done. I am in my final months. I can hang on that long.

Dying with any organization takes a lot of preparation. There are phone calls to be made, details to check on, a will to be made. I have to check on my life insurance coverages and beneficiaries. I have to make sure everyone is taken care of. I make a death binder for Faith that includes all my financial information. It includes my checking, savings, and retirement accounts as well as the telephone and account numbers for each.

So much work. There are advantages, I guess, to being killed suddenly and by complete surprise. You don't have to worry about any of this, but I'm willing to do the leg work. It will be worth it. Besides, it will be the last work I ever have to do. The finish line is close and that gives me strength.

As I wait for my death, the only thing that dampens my excitement is the oppressive weight of depression that has not eased. At work I am barely holding on. I am unsure if I can make it until October. The desire to take matters into my own hands is almost irresistible. Suicide, however, presents its own problems and they are not small.

I am aware that most life insurance policies include some sort of suicide clause stating that benefits will not be paid out if the policy holder's death was a suicide. It figures. Everybody is looking for a loophole. My own suicide would leave the people that I love in a horrible financial mess. It didn't seem fair. Neither have I sorted out what suicide would do to my relationship with God. No. Better to wait.

Depression can make everything so bleak and painful that nothing else matters but ending the misery. When it reaches a certain critical level there is no amount of reasoning or logic that can dissuade a person with a firm suicidal ideation. I could feel my own depression reaching this point of no return.

One afternoon after work, sometime late in July, I pull into a parking spot outside of a local sporting goods store fully intent on buying a handgun. I know my record is clean and with no more than a few hundred-dollar charge to my credit card and a three-day waiting period, I could have the means to my own end. I might not even have to wait. I don't know how these things work.

I don't go in, but I sit in the car for more than 30 minutes considering the ramifications. In the end, it is again the fear for my family that causes me to back out and drive away. I am afraid that if I am in possession of a gun I'll be unable to resist using it. There is a very tiny shred of myself lying somewhere deep that still wants help and if I am dead it will be too late to get it.

It is this shred of who I used to be that encourages me to try one last time to find a psychiatrist within my hospital system. As luck would have it, I find out that the clinic has just hired a new doctor. Her name is Dr. Douglas and she will be coming on staff soon. Because she is new she has no patients and therefore, as long as I pass a screening by the other psychiatrists, I can get in. I pass the screening and the appointment is scheduled for the beginning of October... more than two months away. Good thing it's not an emergency. Oh wait. It is.

# Chapter 33

# The Man in the Moon

The final months are the most difficult. I fluctuate between wanting to die and wanting to hold on till my appointment in October. Several times at work I come within an inch of going to my charge nurse and telling her in private that I am depressed to such an extent that I am honestly afraid of what I might do.

I take to wearing my green corduroy barn coat from the winter because it makes me feel a little better. It's like wearing a tiny dark room and that's pretty much the only place I want to be. But it is August and over a hundred degrees out so it's not a perfect solution. My options, however, are limited. I wear the coat driving. I wear it working. I wear it sleeping.

In late August I spend a Saturday night painting. A half-finished portrait has been sitting untouched on my easel for months so I decide to finish it. Nothing has helped my depression so far. Maybe a distraction and a dose of sleep deprivation will.

I have read that sleep deprivation can sometimes make depression disappear almost overnight. When it works it is only temporary. Once a person begins to sleep again the depression will return. It is risky with my history. Sleep deprivation could bring on a mania. Even mania sounds preferable to the depression that's grinding me to pieces right now. I'm willing to chance it.

It's only one night but maybe it will help. If I can just find something to push me the last month and a half, I'll make it to see this psychiatrist yet. Otherwise I'm finished. If my former lover is right, I'm finished anyway and none of this is going to matter. Whatever. Either way.

I don't make it the entire night. By 3:30 I am exhausted and the whole plan begins to seem ludicrous. I clean my brushes and go outside to sit on the steps in front of my house. I decide to finish the last of my iced tea there and then go to bed. There is something deeply peaceful about the earliest morning hours when the whole world is still sleeping. It's private…safe. This morning, once again, proves my assessment.

The air is humid. I listen to the sounds of the night, the crickets, the occasional passing of a car through the nearby intersection, the cycling on and off of air-conditioning units from neighboring houses. The sky is dotted with stars and the moon is bright, not full but large. A warm breeze rustles my hair and the leaves in the big tree next door. I look up at the moon and am somewhat surprised to see a familiar smiling face looking down at me. Well I'll be damned, the Man in the Moon.

I want to laugh, the image is so irrational. I blink my eyes but it doesn't go away. He's still there. It's the same face I remember from children's stories that my mother read to me when I was small. And it's the most comforting thing I have seen in months.

I'm pretty sure I'm hallucinating again. If it hadn't happened to me in the past I might be more disturbed by that fact. Besides, there is a big difference between interdimensional beings who want to kill me and the Man in the Moon.

I have heard that sometimes stoned people enjoy their hallucinations, aware all the while that what they are seeing is not real. Maybe this is how they feel. It is not frightening. I understand that there is no Man in the Moon and yet... there he is.

He begins to talk to me. I cannot hear him. I decide that must have something to do with the two hundred thousand odd miles separating us. He keeps talking though. It begins to feel awkward. Can he not see that I have no idea what he's saying? I smile at him and shrug. I point at my ear and shake my head apologetically. He is not discouraged. He goes right on talking.

I feel bad. What can I do though? I can't hear what he's saying. I lie back on the sidewalk and cup my head in my hands. I look at the stars. I look at the lights of a distant airplane. I look anywhere but at the Man. What, is he blind or something? He must be able to see that I'm not even paying attention to him? What is he going on about?

Although I try, I cannot ignore him for long. Are you

kidding? It's the Man in the Moon! This is amazing! He is just right there, as clear as he was in the pages of my childhood nursery rhymes. I feel like a kid again. Okay, I think to myself and look back at him. Give it to me again, this time so I can understand it. I see him take a breath and then he tries.

He annunciates very slowly and deliberately in an exaggerated parody of speech. I try to read his lips but I'm still not getting it. I sit up again and concentrate on his mouth with all my focus. Still nothing.

The Man is patient. I'll give him that. He does not get frustrated. He just keeps trying like he has all the time in the moon. After several more fruitless tries, he shortens his message to the barest essential element, the one idea above all others that he wants me to understand. I can see that it contains just three words but I still can't figure it out.

I remember watching *Wheel of Fortune* with my parents when I was in high school. My parents were phenomenal at it. I stunk...and stink. They could solve the puzzles within the first few letters. I could have all but the last letters and still be stumped. The Man in the Moon should be talking to my parents, not me.

I give up. I am getting drowsy and want to sleep. I gulp down the dregs of my iced tea and stand. I apologize to the Man in the Moon and feel silly for doing it. He is a hallucination...isn't he? I tell him we can try again tomorrow but I need to get some sleep. He is insistent though and continues repeating his message to me even as I turn and walk back into the house. Two days later I solve the puzzle.

I am at work when it happens and it hits me like a Nolan Ryan wild pitch to the side of my head.

"You did it." That's what the Man in the Moon was trying to tell me. I can see his exaggerated lip movements forming the words. "You—did—it." I smile and shake my head. So simple. And yet everything makes sense to me now. This may be the single most important thing anything anyone has ever told me. Then answer to how I die.

Everything is connected. It just takes the right perspective to see it. The dream where I am killed on a roller coaster was a premonition. What could be more obvious? It was not meant to be taken literally. The sleeping mind construes certain ideas and blends them with others. It meanders. Still, its foreshadowing of an actual event was accurate. I will soon die and it will come as a result of a head trauma. Beautiful.

This fact was further verified by the spirit of my dead lover who assured me that my death was coming soon. I am nearly done on earth and have only to wait until October. Then I can rest and we will be reunited. That's what she was telling me. And I'm pretty sure I can trust the spirit of my dead lover.

I spent a lot of time speculating on how it's going to happen. Because I am young...ish and healthy, an incurable disease does not fit. I could, I suppose, have a massive heart attack or stroke. It's possible at my age but also seems unlikely. It's more probable that it will be something sudden, the result of some kind of trauma. My money has been on a car wreck. And that is as good a way as any I figure, a means to an end. The Man in the Moon changed that though. Now I know for sure. It is suicide after all. I should have known.

It fits. The head trauma it will involve could come from an impact, one caused by jumping from a great height but I know it won't. It can really only mean one thing in my opinion, a gunshot wound. The day I sat in the parking lot outside the sporting goods store comes back to me. Another of fate's subtle clues?

My life has been bouncing along like a train on the tracks all along...or a roller coaster. I only thought I was making decisions, deciding outcomes. It was already set, though, all of it, including the end. Even The Man in the Moon knows how this ends and he's guiding me home.

"You did it," he told me. Past tense. To him it had already happened in the future. There is no way to change it and I have no desire to. There are still a few plans to make, the where and when of it all, a few more loose ends to tie up and then I am ready.

One of the first things I do is to double check on my finances. I assume that I will not be able to count on my life insurance to pay out so instead try to calculate how much my savings, retirement, and Social Security benefits will pay out to my family. The amounts are more than I thought but still disappointing.

To my surprise I discover on yet another Google search that some life insurance plans do indeed pay out partial or even full benefits in cases of suicide. I call my own insurance provider that same afternoon to find out their policy concerning suicide. The woman on the phone sounds somewhat alarmed at my question and is reluctant to answer but she has little choice. I am the customer and I am paying for the policy. It is my right to know.

She confirms to my delight that the policy will in fact pay out first partial benefits, then once I have held the policy for two years, it will pay out in full.

"Can you tell me when my policy will reach its two-year anniversary?" I ask her.

She hesitates.

"Ma'am?"

There is a faint sigh on the line, then, "October 17th of this year."

October. I smile. Fate.

# Chapter 34

# By My Fingertips

September passes. It is awful but I am close. My memory is getting spotty. Sometimes I pass my exit on the freeway and get confused. Things don't look familiar and it takes me several minutes to figure out where I am and make my way back.

It happens in the hospital as well. The elevator doors open and I get off on the wrong floor. That's all it takes for the whole framework of my world to collapse. I can't figure out where I am or what I'm doing. Everything goes, not just what floor I'm on. All of it.

Where am I? Is this a hospital? Is it my hospital? Am I working? Am I coming or going? How do I find my way out? What's going on?

I make plans to kill myself. I decide on a hotel room because I don't want my family's home to become a scene from a horror movie. I don't want them to have to clean my blood and brain matter from the walls.

I decide on October 26th for my last day of life. The

weekend immediately following the two year anniversary of my life insurance will be my birthday weekend. It would be fitting, I admit, but there will be expectations that weekend, people to fake-smile at, small talk to force. It might be hard to break away for an overnight at a hotel. Easier to wait one more week then slip away when things are quieter. Yes. The 26th is perfect. Only a few weeks left.

My problem so far this year has been an inability to care or feel. Now things begin to change slightly but not in a way that encourages me. It is awkward and unpleasant. I can feel nothing and then something small will break my heart and my eyes will begin to well with tears as if I might cry right there on the spot. A song, a moment…sometimes nothing at all. Maybe I'm just getting nostalgic because I'm nearing the end.

One day at work I see a woman standing at the bedside of her mother. Her mother is dying. Like me, she will not see Christmas this year. The old woman is at peace with it but her daughter is in agony. Her daughter doesn't know how to let go. The mother doesn't know how to help her. The two of them just stay that way, side by side, each loving the other but locked on their own paths, no way to alter them. The poignancy of the moment is so scorching that I have to turn away.

There comes an evening, one of the last before my hospitalization, when I am feeling even lower than low, when simply drawing breath has become a job of monumental accomplishment and I manage to text Brian. It is a chilling text that I will not even recall sending. I will discover it only months later in my text logs and realize why he called me back within minutes.

"Nothing is ever going to be enough. I don't want to do this anymore. I'm so very tired. I've had enough," I say.

We talk, sort of. Or at least that's what Brian will later tell me. Mostly he talks. I am unable. I won't remember the few things that I say or my voice cracking with emotion when I try. I won't remember that I barely speak loud enough for him to hear me or the long pauses it takes for me to form responses. I am glad for that small mercy.

Out of concern, Brian must have alerted our mutual friends because I begin to receive other calls and texts from people I have not heard from in months or even years. I do not respond to them. I am in no condition and have no desire to do so. I'd sooner compete in a triathlon.

I am aware that the date of my upcoming appointment with Dr. Douglas is going to arrive before the date of my life insurance's two year anniversary and soon to follow death. That's sort of awkward but I decide to keep the appointment anyway. Why not? Plan B, the plan for help, it appears will get its shot before plan A, the plan for suicide, but whatever. I don't care a whit about the outcome of my life.

Maybe Dr. Douglas can help me. It seems like sort of a 90-yard Hail Mary pass into dense coverage but what the hell. If she pulls it off that's fine I suppose. I'm open-minded. To tell the truth, I not only expect her to fail but I'd really prefer her to. My final days have already been laid out.

Life beyond October has not existed for me for months, not since I was told it would be the month of my death. I have made no plans. I have let go of my future. I have made arrangements. I have arrived. Peace is within my reach. My mood lifts ever so slightly. I compliment my co-workers and tell my family that I love them. It will not be long now.

October 2nd, the day of my appointment with Dr. Douglas arrives. I work, though I have no idea how I am still doing so. Faith, who has been worried sick about me, leaves work early to accompany me to the doctor's office. I have hidden as much as I can from her but she is still terrified. She knows all too well about the power of a major depressive episode from harrowing personal experiences of her own.

I pace in the waiting room while Faith reads a magazine. I know why I am nervous. Talking about my feelings, revealing my weakness and most humiliating failings is always a shame fest. It never gets easier, no matter how many times I've had to do it.

The door to the back offices opens and a woman calls my name. Dr. Douglas. She is younger than I expect and tall. She has a pleasant face and a pixie cut of dark brown hair. We shake hands and I follow her back to her office. We talk, which is to say, I assume we talk. I remember very little about what I say. I think it may be everything. I promised myself I would. I would not hold back. If I was going to give this a chance it had to be an honest chance.

More than an hour passes while I presumably outline the past year and the plan to end my life. When next I am aware of my surroundings, Faith is there with me. I'm not sure when she came in but she is now seated next to me. She is nodding at Dr. Douglas. Dr. Douglas is talking to both of us but more to Faith than to me. That's strange.

"Mmmm…hmmm. Mmmm…hmmm," Faith is saying. Her voice is strained, her expression tense. She is trying to appear calm but there are too many "mmm hmmms." Her mind is trying to process what she is being told but it has snagged on something.

What are we talking about? I struggle to refocus. Dr. Douglas's voice becomes words again. The hospital? Me? An inpatient? Wait. Are you kidding? A psych ward? Is that what this is about? I just thought I was going to go back on medication.

I can't go to the hospital. I have to work. I'm refinancing our house and am closing this week. I have to buy a hand-gun. The 26th is just around the corner. Tomorrow is a busy day at work and we will already be a nurse short. I have to…I can't…impossible.

I cut in, try to explain why this will never do. Dr. Douglas listens as I present all of my irrelevant arguments to her like little plastic bags of evidence to a jury. She is unmoved by any of it.

She tells me again that she is firm about this and is not budging. She gives me time for things to sink in. Finally I give up. I look at Dr. Douglas. I look at Faith. I look out the window. I let out a long sigh and then release everything. I know she's right. I know I'm very sick. I can't fight things anymore. I am not safe.

# Chapter 35

# Surrender

**Hospitalization—October 2013**. Sitting at that table in the day room with Faith filling out intake paperwork is one of the last things I remember for several days. During the months leading up to my hospitalization I did everything I could to manage my symptoms on my own and hide them from the world. I created a formidable dam to hold back the rising waters of my depression. As time went on, however, my dam began to fail. Crazy began sloshing over the top and spewing between the cracks.

I worked night and day to hold it together, exhausting myself in the process. It was a hopeless task, but there was nothing else to do. This must have been how I managed to work so near to my admission. The dam was still holding.

I was at least as sick as the patients I was trying to take care of but apparently just functional enough to get by. I was still keeping all the balls in the air. As far as I know I was keeping all the balls in the air. Let's hope none of my charts from that period of my life are ever audited. A catastrophic failure of my dam was imminent though. It was just a matter of time.

When I was driven to the hospital that afternoon I was already letting go. I made it. Help was on the scene. I knew I was safe. I was so exhausted. Now in the care of professionals, I can't fight it anymore. Relieved to give up any last pretenses, I abandon my ill-fated dam for good.

Left unattended, the dam disintegrates almost immediately and I am too numb to care. There is no noise when it finally goes. There should be. There should be an explosion that shakes the ground as it crumbles but there is nothing, not a peep, no sign to mark its passing. No one looks up. I am the only one who sees it.

I see the irresistible force of 10 months of depression slam through my defenses and come roaring toward me. I don't put up my hands. I don't even take a breath. I simply close my eyes and wait for it to break over me. When it hits, everything goes black.

\* \* \*

Both depression and mania can affect memory, punching gaping holes in it like a hellacious night of binge drinking. Nevertheless, such a long and complete gap for me is a new and unsettling experience. When my memory next begins to flicker to life and retain fleeting bits of information it is three days later.

None of my doctors seem surprised or bothered by my memory loss when later I mention it to them. They tell me it is very common for patients as ill as I am to lose whole swaths of time. They go on to reassure me that my memory will get better when I do.

I have little choice but to take the doctors' word on that but am happy to report, they do turn out to be right. Still, those first three days in the hospital as well as the rest of the countless other blank outs of time while I am there are lost to me forever. Then again, not everything in life is worth remembering.

My journal begins out of necessity. I am absolutely unable to remember anything that is happening to me. Who I have met, where I am, or what I am doing there. I take notes in an effort to try and keep up. Before long though, what starts as a jumble of jotted down facts and reminders, such as my room number and my doctors' names, becomes a readable journal.

I start to include my thoughts and feelings about what is happening. They may have encouraged us to do this some-time in those first few days as a type of therapy, but if they did I have no memory of it. I find only that now my notes have become a journal which even includes day headings to the extent that I knew any. When I look back though at the few disconnected notes from the lost days, they jog nothing in my mind. If not for seeing my own handwriting I would think they were someone else's memories. There are not many entries. I was not, it seems, doing much writing, or anything else those first few days.

According the medical records which I later obtain, I spent the bulk of my time curled in the fetal position on a chair in the day room neither speaking nor moving. I suppose it's a given to say it, but there's no man alive that wants to hear he has spent time in the fetal position (we'll call it fetaling) in public. Alas...the following is a recreation of those first days and the ones that followed based on the journal I kept while there.

# Chapter 36

# Black Out

**Wednesday through Saturday**—My memory is Swiss cheese. When I talk I have the distinct feeling that I may already have said whatever it is I'm saying either to the person I'm speaking to, or perhaps to someone else. Wait, who *is* the person I'm speaking to?

Who are you? Are you my doctor? Have we already met? I can't tell whether I've met everyone here or haven't met anyone. Things seem both vaguely familiar and not familiar at all. I am lost.

The unit consists of a multipurpose day room, a nurses' station, a quiet room, an electroconvulsive treatment room (shock treatment), and a hallway of patient rooms. The enormous day room serves as a recreational area (if you can call puzzles and TV recreation), a dining area, and a visiting area. Not only are these features of the unit not initially evident to me, but neither is the purpose of the unit itself. I am easily confused.

Periodically I think I am in some type of school and can't

219

figure out why I am here. I decide it must be a school for the arts. A time or two I mistake it for an airport as well. Nothing is sticking. I am forever trying to orient myself with no prior memories on which to base my deductions. I have to "discover" my room each time I go there, checking the room numbers and studying the plaques outside of each door hoping something will look familiar. When I find one I think may be mine, I push open the door just a crack and peer inside. Each time I see my things on the desk it is a small victory.

On two separate occasions I get trapped in my bathroom because I can't figure out that the door pulls open instead of pushes. Both times only my pride keeps me from pulling the emergency cord and calling for assistance. I'm not this stupid. Can depression really affect a person like this?

My doctors have to tell me who they are and what their names are over and over again and whole sections of my day drop from my memory like chunks of the California coast into the sea. They're just gone. I have no idea what happened during those periods.

It's as if my memory has become one of those classified documents that has been redacted by the government. One where half of the text has been blacked out with a Sharpie or something. Sometimes it is only sentences, other times paragraphs, and sometimes whole pages.

When I try to make sense of things by stringing my memories together the remaining portions make no sense. Too much has been lost, obliterated under black ink. I have only fading snapshot memories, random and disconnected.

They are elusive and ethereal and I fear if I don't write them down they will fade like dreams in the morning light.

I remember sitting on the floor in the hall with another patient, a tall man who looks like the actor Craig T. Nelson from the old TV show *Coach*. Sometimes he is violent but he was okay at that moment. I was listening to him tell me about an argument he got in with one of the nurses. It felt like we are a couple of third graders complaining about one of our teachers.

In another memory, I sat by myself on the floor trying to put a puzzle together. It was a struggle but I managed to complete a 25-piece cartoon scene of some barnyard chicks hatching from eggs. I decided to try a bigger puzzle. It was a scene from the movie *Toy Story* and had maybe a hundred pieces or so. I thought I could at least get it started.

I gave it a go but was nowhere near up to the challenge. I was unable to connect even two pieces of the puzzle…I was in way over my head. I returned the pieces to the box and replaced it on the shelf where I got it. Then I shambled over to the couch to take a nap. The puzzles had exhausted me both mentally and physically.

I have yet another unpleasant memory of being upset in a group therapy session. I was alternately tearful and angry. I went on about something but no one could understand me. They allowed me to cry and shout and whatever…God knows. I guess they'd seen that sort of thing before.

I know I was still feeling low and suicidal as hell but as I struggle now to recall what I was feeling in those first days it's not sadness that I remember as much as profound confusion. All my higher brain function had shorted out. I was like a big toddler. I suppose that's why people have to be locked up. When it's that bad you just can't take care of yourself anymore. It hasn't gotten much better either.

Twice and possibly counting, I have had to be Haldol'd for trying to gnaw off my right index finger, or so they tell me. The finger, to my knowledge, has done nothing to me for which I should be harboring a grudge. Nevertheless.

My finger bears definite evidence of some determined gnawing between the second and third knuckles but the bone must have been harder than I anticipated. It remains stubbornly in place not even broken let alone severed clean off. It's just as well.

I lose things constantly, my shoes, my handouts from group, my book, my glasses, etc. I find it works better to carry everything on me at all times. I am a Sherpa loaded for expedition.

I am able to pack along so many of my possessions because I am once again wearing, in addition to a pair of pajama pants that grow dirtier by the day, my green corduroy barn coat, my depression coat, the one I took to wearing back in August. The coat's curious design includes more pockets than one might find in three coats. It is a little bit like wearing a storage and filing cabinet around, and I have not taken it off since my admission.

I wear the coat when I am feeling low because it provides a comforting barrier between myself and the world. In truth, if I could, I would probably wear a cardboard refrigerator box with two eye holes cut in the side. This obviously being out of the question I settle for my green corduroy coat. It is the next best thing. So although I would wear the coat anyway, the numerous pockets are a convenient bonus as they allow me to carry nearly everything that I could conceivably find myself in need of. It is a shoplifter's dream coat.

Now as I wobble unsteadily around the psych ward trying to adjust to the new medicine I've been put on, I am packing along with me at least two different books, my journal, a pencil, several handouts, and an apple. I had a pair of reading glasses but I lost them, yet again. And I had a banana at some point. I may have lost it too…or eaten it. I can't remember.

The coat is a drab green which fits my mood nicely. If it was a bright color, it would never do, even given its abundance of pockets. Cheerful colors, like light itself right now are an unwelcome assault on my senses. Thankfully, however, it is dull and drab like myself. And when I need to I can pull myself nearly entirely inside it, legs and all. I tuck myself into a corner of the couch. I draw my knees up and the coat folds over me leaving nothing behind but a dull corduroy lump. I am invisible.

Occasionally I try to read but have no more success than when I tried to put the *Toy Story* puzzle together. Reading has always been a sanctuary for me. Books are doorways to places where I don't have to think. All the challenges are somebody else's to deal with as are all the consequences. All I have to do as the reader is enjoy the ride. And rereading my old books always feels like going home again. It is a comfort I need more than ever in here so I carry two of my favorites with me wherever I go. I suppose Faith brought them in for me at some point but so far all they have done is frustrate me.

Each time I open one of the books, I find myself reading and rereading the same paragraph, sometimes the same sentence. Nothing happens. No meaning. I just can't catch the thread of the language. I can't escape. It's as though I am trying to read a book written in Russian...or maybe one about Hobbits. I try for a few minutes, then get discouraged and put it back into one of my many pockets.

One of the casualties of a really profound depression is the ability to concentrate. When we read, our eyes move across the page. Each word is read and understood not only as an individual word but in context with the words that came before it. It is only with the context of the entire string of words that we can extract the complex ideas being communicated and follow a running train of thought.

To accomplish this, our brains use a working memory, like a computer does. When my concentration is severely impaired, it is as though my working memory has been wiped out. I understand the individual words my eyes are moving over but the ones before it keep dropping out of memory so there is never any context for what I'm reading. The result is that things make no sense. It's all just a bunch of unrelated words.

It is the same when I am listening to someone. If their statements are very short, I can understand them. If they start to expound about anything we're both toast. I can understand the individual words they're saying but can't hold enough of them in my working memory to relate them together. There is no context and nothing makes sense so I just tune it all out. Interestingly, the same thing happens if I get too manic.

# Chapter 37

# Zero to Sixty

**Sunday 10/6/2013**—Faith came today smelling of Perry Ellis 360 and looking like the picture of mental stability. She has struggled with chronic depression herself and knows too well about stormy moods. We make quite a pair. But today she is the sane one, the put together one, the one getting buzzed in as a visitor and me the one in my pajamas and corduroy coat at 2:00 in the afternoon. Ahhh, well.

The visit doesn't go well. We have a couples' therapy session, an included option if we want it, like a free massage or a ball cap with a psych ward logo on it. Faith accepts it on our behalf. During the session we discuss a variety of topics but we both know where this is going, where it has to go. Finally, to the dismay of all involved, we go there.

The relationship between Faith and my daughter Cornelia has been the one hurdle in our marriage we have not been able to clear. Blended families are faced with challenges that can erode even the strongest resolve. In our case, the problem has always revolved around Faith's difficulty accepting Cornelia into our new family. For Faith it may be a simple jealousy issue, causing her to react negatively to a perceived threat for my affection. It might also be a deep-seated instinct that causes her to view Cornelia as an interloper like a cuckoo's parasitic offspring deposited in her nest. She knows her feelings are unfair but has been unable to keep them affecting her opinion and treatment of Cornelia. My attempts to protect Cornelia and to change Faith's mind has fueled some epic arguments.

The arguments, which have not been a few, inevitably leave Faith feeling blamed and attacked unfairly by an over-protective father and me feeling caught between my wife and daughter, unable to make things better for either of them. The stress of this issue has contributed, without a doubt, to periodic depressions in both of us. At times I am amazed, despite the deep abiding love we share for one other, that Faith and I have been able to stay together this long.

There is nothing that will ignite an argument faster for us than rehashing this issue for the thousandth time. We both know it. We avoid talking about it like we avoid opening the door to Mormons.

We have both lost this battle too many times not to know that this is an invitation to misery. The only things we have to show for our countless attempts at finding a solution are emotional scars atop emotional scars. The price we will pay for once again broaching this poisonous topic will be all the feelings of amiability, affection, and warmth between us. Still, an opportunity to have this thorn in our relationship re-examined by fresh eyes…professional eyes, is too valuable to pass up. Maybe, just maybe, this new therapist can help us.

The result is sadly what it always is, a spectacular failure. In the end, the therapist just stares at us stupefied. If he has any idea how to begin to defuse this situation, he doesn't share it with us. He too seems astonished that we have remained married for nine years. This part is not such a mystery though. Love as strong as ours is hard to give up on. No one ever claimed we were functional.

When Faith leaves, she is stiff, tight-lipped and aloof. She gives me a quick passionless kiss and says she will return tomorrow. She continues to play the good wife for anyone watching until they mercifully buzz her out. I know she needs her space and am not surprised when she doesn't call to say goodnight.

Despite the disappointment of Faith's wintery departure, my mood begins to rise. Throughout the afternoon it drifts lazily higher and higher like a balloon slipped from the grasp of a child. It feels good, amazingly good, like waking up healthy one morning after a long and terrible cold.

One of the girls on the unit named Hilary is having the rather depressing experience of celebrating her birthday as a patient on the psych floor. I draw her a "card" on a dry erase board that sits unused in the day room and get all the patients to sign it. I tell her I would have gone out to CVS to get her a real card except that I am currently under house arrest. She says that it's okay and that she likes this one better anyway.

Another patient that I have warmed to is named Gwen. Gwen is a woman with an enormous heart and currently a severe depression. She is one birthday shy of seventy but looks at least ten years younger. She is one of two self-called grandmas that took me under their proverbial wing when I first came to the unit and was so profoundly depressed that I could barely speak. It is a kindness for which I will always be in her debt. Now that I am able to interact I find that Gwen and I are cut from the same rather colorful cloth. We share our stories, encourage each other, and forge an instant friendship.

Gwen and I feel terrible that Hilary has to celebrate her birthday like this and we're determined to do what we can to make things better. We tell Hilary's nurse that today is her birthday and ask if she could please order her a cake or a birthday balloon or something. She assures us that she will try but we have our doubts. She has that look that says, "Yes, yes. We'll see, okay? Now you two run along." So when evening rolls around and still nothing has come, Gwen and I, scheming like a couple of trolls, decide to take matters into our own hands.

From one of the two patient phones I get and outside line then call back into the hospital. As a former employee I still remember the hospital exchange if not any actual departmental numbers. After a couple of tries I reach a person who, believing I am another staff member, thoughtfully transfers me to Nutrition Services.

When a woman picks up in Nutrition Services, I say, "Hi, I'm a nurse calling, from the fourth floor," which technically is true. "I ordered a birthday cake for one of my patients yesterday but haven't received it. Would you mind checking on it for me?"

The woman hesitates. "Uh, we don't really do things like that for patients," she says.

I push a little. "Well, I'm pretty sure we do because I have ordered one before and it wasn't a problem." This is obviously a lie. An entire cake may have been a bit too ambitious I realize but I was hoping to get something everyone could share.

We end up bargaining down to a cupcake. We'll just have to forget sharing this time. She sighs and says she will talk to her supervisor. She asks me for the patient's name and since I don't know Hilary's last name, I just give the woman her room number. This is written on a list posted by the phones. It must suffice because she grunts in annoyance and hangs up.

I am surprised she was so resistant. A single dessert doesn't seem like an unreasonable request on someone's birthday. I really thought they did stuff like that. Maybe that was Olive Garden. Whatever.

Resistant or not though, about 10 minutes later the back door buzzes open and someone from Nutrition Services walks onto the floor with a chocolate cupcake on a tray. There is no candle on it, presumably because one of us would use it to set ourselves on fire, but it's a cupcake none the less. Gwen and I share a high five. Once again, it feels like we are a couple of kids in school.

Hilary sits in a recliner by herself in front of the TV and

takes her time relishing every last bite of the cupcake. She may even have smiled. It would be the first time I have seen her smile since I have been here. Happy birthday, Hil!

As the evening wears on, my mood continues its steady ascent. I find myself suddenly not only ready to talk to people again but desperate to. This leads to most excellent conversations with nearly every patient on the unit. I come to the conclusion that mental patients are among the most interesting, and approachable group of people around. This view, I admit, is probably not widely held.

At 10:00 p.m. when the regulations require that the TVs be turned off, I am prattling on a mile a minute with an entourage of patients and nurses alike. They gather around me like moons caught in my gravitational field. I am leading a scintillating round table discussion that touches on everything from reincarnation to the Christian implications of suicide. I feel a genuine love for everyone in the room and it seems contagious. Even people I have never before heard speak are joining in.

With the TVs off though and most of the patients' evening meds beginning to kick in, the round table finally breaks up and patients begin drifting back to their rooms. Fascinating bunch, but these mental patients but have no stamina. I by contrast, am wide awake.

By 10:30 I am the only one left but feel too energized to sleep and so I pace. It feels good to move although I am still a little unsteady. I am still getting used to the new meds they put me on here, one of which is lithium. Lithium can cause dizziness. It makes me feel like I have had too many glasses of wine, sort of off balance and uncoordinated but without any of the pleasurable effects of a buzz.

They say I will get used to it, maybe. For now I wobble around like a colt on spindly legs, back and forth. I find that as I pick up some speed it's even kind of fun especially when I U-turn at the ends of the room to come back. It's a little bit like a carnival ride I decide…admittedly not a ride that would have much of a wait to get on.

When I have had enough of the pacing ride for the time being, I sit down at a table, jiggle my leg furiously, and dash off a quick five or six pages in my journal. That done, I head over to the windows for a look at the city lights. I find to my delight that it's nearing Christmas time.

The traffic lights change from red to yellow to green and the twinkling head lights and tail lights of passing cars all have a cheery festive feel to them. Peace on earth and good-will toward men. I smile.

I think of the Christmas story. I wonder why there is no Christmas tree up in here. Wait. Christmas? Unghh. My heart sinks. I realize that this all means I will have to live through another Christmas. Another Christmas with its buying and thinking and decorating and cooking and wrapping and social gatherings and short sunless days.

I cringe and shake Christmas from my head before it can bring me down any lower. I've had it with low. I've been choking on low. But I am feeling better now, much better. I chuckle quietly to myself. My meds shouldn't be working this fast but I'm not complaining. It almost feels like I'm getting manic but that can't be. No. I will be getting out of here soon, I'm certain. I move away from the windows then pace a few more laps, just to get my groove back.

When I look up from my pacing, I see that it is after midnight. Sleep is important to the staff here. I have gathered that much. They are always asking us how much we got the night before. I don't want to raise any suspicions so I turn in my pencil to the nurses' station for the night and pad off to my room, which, I realize now with satisfaction, I am able to find with breathtaking ease. Ha! And exiting my bathroom, I might also add, is a snap.

After getting ready for bed I slip under the covers but sleep does not come for me. Instead I lay in bed flexing and unflexing my feet and watching the chaotic images in my mind. When I get manic and close my eyes, I see either a high speed slide show of random and usually unrelated images which my brain sorts through at dizzying speeds. Other times it plays weird silent movies that look mashups of short film clippings all spliced together and run at triple speed. No sound.

Tonight it's the slide show and apparently there's an animal theme. Each slide is a close up of some part of an animal, possum teeth, snake ribs, mouse paw, wolf eye, etc. Not disturbing just bizarre, and of course, going really really fast. It becomes a game for me to try and guess the animals as the close-ups of their body parts flash by before the image changes. Rabbit. Iguana. Lady bug. I'm pretty good at this. Pig. Sloth. Pass…no, wait. House cat!

It occurs to me that I should probably be grateful that the show has not included any slides of spider parts, as I am a huge arachnophobe. No sooner does the thought come to me than my mind does just that showing tarantulas and huge South American tree spiders that eat birds and clip onto your face. This is a highly disturbing content switch to say the least. But you know what? I don't have to play this game.

I open my eyes and sit up on the side of my bed. I am of course, still wearing my corduroy barn coat. At first I found it uncomfortable to wear in bed. It kept binding me up when I rolled from side to side. That is until I discovered that it works much better, at least when sleeping, if I wear it backwards. This is how I have it on now.

I decide to have a look at the view outside my window. Although I have been here for many days, I have spent them in a fog of depressed disinterest. It never entered my mind to open my curtains and look out of the window.

There is a couch built into the wall directly in front of the window. It makes it hard to reach the curtains. I could lean over the couch, plant one hand on the sill for balance, and use the other to part the curtains at the bottom. That way I could get a glimpse through the wedge of light. Nah. That won't do. I am wide awake. My mind is alert, buzzing with curiosity, all the little synapses glittering and shivering with efficiency. I want the full Monty so I stand up on the couch cushions and snap open the drapes with a dramatic flourish like I'm Pip in Mrs. Havisham's crumbling old mansion.

It is at this precise moment that the night nurse pushes open my door with a flashlight to perform one of her many nightly bed checks on me. There I am in the pitch dark, standing on the couch with my arms outstretched, and my coat on backwards. I turn part ways to face her. We stare at each other an awkward minute. I lower my arms.

"Evenin," I say conversationally. I am a Southern gentleman smoking a pipe on my veranda greeting a passerby on a warm Kentucky evening.

She blinks. "Everything okay?"

"Yep. Yep. Everything's good. Thanks."

"You, uh, just opening the drapes?"

I nod. "Yep. Just opening the drapes." I remain where I am.

She nods then begins to back out of the room. "Call if you need anything."

"Will do," I reply. "Thanks." The door clicks shut. I sigh. This will not look good. Oh well. What's done is done, I think as I make myself comfortable on the window sill.

The view is magnificent.

It's an alley.

There are several steam pipes on the roof below my window. The sight of them makes me think of the rooftops of Victorian London.

It looks nothing like the rooftops of Victorian London.

I picture Dick Van Dyke standing down there singing "Chim Chim Cher-ee." I hum little bit of "Chim Chim Cher-ee." There is also a postcard perfect parking garage just across the alley from me. Do they put parking garages on postcards? Well, they should. This one is an architectural masterpiece. I think it would have impressed Thomas Jefferson.

It would impress no one.

I picture Batman running across the roof top parking level and flinging himself off the edge. He would soar out across the gap and just catch the lip of the next building with one hand. In a fluid motion, he would vault himself onto the roof of that building and disappear into the shadows. I hum a little bit of the Batman theme.

From where I sit I can see the lights of Reunion Tower, the famous ball on the Dallas skyline. The lights around the ball blink on and off. It is a complex code based on combinations of color and timing. I decipher it nimbly in my head. It is a Christmas greeting meant especially for me.

It has nothing whatever to do with me...and it's October.

I watch hypnotized for a few minutes or an hour before returning to bed to flex and unflex my feet some more. I leave the curtains open so that I will be able to see the sunrise.

Checks.

Checks.

Checks.

I am awake for them all. What a mind-bendingly long night, I think in annoyance, flexing my feet. When will it ever end?

# Chapter 38

# Flipped

**Monday 10/7/2013**—Just as first light is turning the sky from black to gray that morning, I am saved from my boredom by the phlebotomist. She has come to draw my lithium level. She swings open the door with a bang right to the stop, pushes in a rattling cart of equipment, flips on the overhead light, and announces herself, "Lab!"

It seems perhaps not the best technique for entering a patient room before sun up. I doubt it has ever gone over well. But today it does! I, unlike your average bleary eyed hospital patient, pop up like a jack-in-the-box, a big smile on my face thrilled to have a visitor. I shuck off my coat and present my arm at once, happy to point out my best veins. I am very helpful. I watch with intense focus as she pushes the needle into my arm and blood fills her tube. Fascinating!

It could not be less fascinating. I myself have performed this procedure thousands of times before. Ahhh, well. I guess it all has to do with perspective.

She withdraws her needle and I hold a tiny square of

gauze over the site until she wraps it with a nonadhesive bandage. She tells me to have a nice day and I assure her I will. As she rattles back out the door, she flips the light off again. I leap out of bed immediately and flip it back on.

Morning at last! Time for a shower. But wait. What's this? No towels? What a nuisance. I throw on my barn coat again, and zip down to the nurses' station. I greet every one of the staff I see along the way.

"Good morning! Good morning! Nice to see you," I beam. "Could I please have some towels? Thank you. Thank you. You're so kind." I take my new towels back down the hall toward my room. When I round the corner and am out of sight of the nurses' station, I give in to giddy temptation and break into a full-on Usain Bolt sprint down the main hall just to feel the speed. I explode into my room grinning like a maniac, which by the way is no coincidence. Dimly, it occurs to me, this may not be a good sign but dammit, it was fun to do.

Once showered, I dress again, for variety's sake I suppose, in my pajamas and barn coat. I brush my teeth and head back out to the day room. My brain is sharp and alert. A keen observer might say, I am concerningly alert.

On the way out the door I snatch up one of the two books that I have with me in the hospital, one about an Alaskan smoke jumper. I am confident that today I will once again be able to understand the content of what I just read. This book, in fact, may not be the best use of my time. I wonder if there are any scientific journals in with those magazines in the day room.

I stuff the smoke jumping book into another of the yawning pockets of my depression coat. Clearly I am no longer depressed but the wisdom of carrying all my possessions around with me is still sound. Walking the short distance back to my room to get my book later if I want to read it would be preposterous. What a waste of pockets like these. I'm not an idiot. I'm not crazy. Clearly.

I eat my breakfast and visit with my groggy friends who are apparently not ready to talk yet which is fine since I do all the talking anyway. After finishing, I clear my tray and offer to clear everyone else's at the table. "You're still eating? Oh, of course. How silly of me not to notice. My apologies."

"I head over to the couch. There I sit and scrawl half a dozen pages in my journal which in my mind has now become a book, a soon to be best-seller. As I write...I rock back and forth.

When I am manic, I stay in constant motion. Unable to sit still, I pace the floor when I'm on my feet or shift my weight back and forth from one foot to the other. If I'm sitting, I might jiggle my leg. If I'm feeling especially jiggly, I jiggle both legs at the same time. I jiggle them together. I jiggle them alternately. Whatever. The dead giveaway that I'm manic is when I begin to rock. It's not a good look.

When I glance up Gwen is there. The staff are sitting her down at a table. She is wearing a hospital gown and looks dazed. I know she has just had her electro convulsive therapy or ECT treatment.

ECT is a once controversial treatment for depression that has been re-embraced by mainstream psychiatry. The technique involves putting a patient to sleep and then sending a low level of electricity into their brain to stimulate a seizure. Why this helps to alleviate the symptoms of depression is anybody's guess. It seems to be akin to hitting the reset button on a computer when you can't clear a glitch. The idea is that when the brain reboots after the seizure, the levels of neurotransmitters will restore themselves to their factory settings.

I learn here that a typical ECT series consists of between eight and twelve treatments. I already know that they are well known for seriously jacking with people's memory, especially their short term memory. Some of their lost memories return in time. Many never do. For this reason, it is primarily used on those patients on whom all other treatments have failed.

I wait for Gwen to orient herself. I've seen her after ECT before and know she will need a little time to readjust to her surroundings. I need to see if she will recognize me and remember that we are friends. Her eyes slowly focus. She sees me. She smiles. Ha! I'm up and bounding across the room in a wink. I flop into a chair next to her and we chat a while or I chat a while. She smiles and nods. She will get a headache later but it hasn't hit yet.

Gwen is leaving the hospital today and both of us are feeling the loss of one another. It's strange how close people can become after a week on a locked psych unit. I suppose it is because we witness such vulnerability in each other. We are all too broken to try and hide it and too much alike to judge each other for it.

Before she leaves, I share lunch with Gwen, her son, and daughter-in-law who have come to pick her up. I have them howling with laughter (or maybe it's just me laughing) and I don't let them get a word in edge-wise. After lunch Gwen and I share an emotional hug. I give her my St. Jude medallion. Outside the hospital I wear the medallion around my neck on a chain. I shouldn't have it in here at all least I kill myself with it, but it got missed during the initial search and seizure and I have kept it hidden ever since, until now.

I secret it into Gwen's hand explaining that St. Jude is the patron saint of hopeless cases and lost causes. I tell her that no matter how awful things may seem at times, there's always hope. If she thinks it is ironic to be getting this message from someone who only a week ago was planning to shoot himself in the head, she doesn't say so.

She accepts the medallion and tells me that she loves me. Oddly it feels genuine and I return the compliment. Then again, we are both a little out of our minds and I am feeling a bit loving toward the whole world. We exchange contact information that I will doubtless misplace and she leaves. I watch her go standing in my pajamas, hospital footies, and ever-present corduroy barn coat.

I miss her immediately but my skyrocketing mood doesn't allow me to dwell on it for more than a minute or two. It doesn't allow me to dwell on anything for more than a minute or two so I dart off to pace, and journal, and jabber on like an auctioneer to anyone I can get to listen or anyone who is just too exhausted to get away from me.

Hilary leaves that same afternoon. When we say our

goodbyes, her husband is with her. I shake his hand.

"Hi. I'm Frank. I'm one of the nurses here," I say with absolute seriousness.

He takes in my get-up and raises a dubious brow. Realizing my mistake, I correct myself.

"I'm sorry," I say. "I meant to say I'm one of the mental patients here."

"He is a nurse though," Hilary offers. Her husband nods and smiles. His teeth look like tiny porcelain soap dishes and I expect to hear a "bing" as the light glints off them. I smile back and excuse myself.

"Gotta jet. I've got group," I say. Group is group therapy and while attendance is not required, it is strongly encouraged by the staff. That's code for, if you don't go, you're not getting out of here. Hilary and I hug. We tell each other to take care and then I am off.

At some point that afternoon, though I can't say when, my attending doctor comes to talk to me. Her name is Dr. Phillips. She talks very slowly or so it seems to me, like I am a child or someone threatening to throw themselves off a ledge. It makes me a little impatient. I want things to move along.

She questions me about my thoughts and my lack of sleep the night before. Each question reminds me of a funny story so I interrupt her and launch into it with gusto. This happens more than a few times. I make her laugh or think I do. Maybe she is just being polite. But each time she redirects my scattered mind back to the topic at hand.

"We think the Zoloft you've been on for depression is

flipping you," she explains. "It's a risk when you have bipolar disorder and take an antidepressant. The antidepressant flips you." She studies my expression gauging my level of comprehension. It's fine.

I am actually already aware of this risk although I had not heard of it happening with Zoloft. It would explain what's been happening to me. It would explain why I feel so good but can't sit still to save my life.

Just the same she adds, "It flips the poles." She points two fingers at me rock paper scissors style and rotates her hand to demonstrate poles flipping. I get it. "It can trigger a manic episode and we want to avoid that," she says.

I like this doctor very much. In fact I like all my doctors here. They are more caring and more professional than any psychiatrists I have met. And not one of them is weird—a common short coming among psychiatric professionals. I know I am in excellent hands and in this moment I feel profoundly grateful that the woman sitting in front of me chose to go into psychiatry. I will do my best to not disappoint her.

She goes on to explain that she is going to increase my dose of lithium. The blood level drawn this morning came back lower than the therapeutic range. She is also changing my antidepressant from Zoloft to a medication called Seroquel.

"Fair enough," I say congenially. "I'm on board."

She smiles at me in a way I have seen before. It's a smile that says she finds my zaniness endearing and wishes me the best. I don't deserve the smile. I know it is not really me she is smiling at.

When I'm manic I can be extremely entertaining. I shine. I'm magnetic. A little bit of mania draws people to me, at least in its early stages it does. I feel a twinge of guilt as she gets up to leave like I am a thief who has just lifted her wrist watch without her knowing it. I wish I was half as entertaining when I was simply me.

And the afternoon wanders into evening. Yowza yowza yowza. I am journaling myself silly and think that the staff will strangle me if I ask them to sharpen my pencil one more time. If they would just give me a pen, I'd be able to leave them alone. Patients aren't allowed to use pens though because obviously we would, again, kill ourselves with them. Why with pens though and not the pencils? I can't say. Administrators.

That evening I am a whirlwind on the unit. I pick things up. I straighten magazines. I launch out of my chair each time the phone rings and race to answer it. Not that anyone is trying to beat me to it.

Most everyone on the unit right now is depressed, except me that is. I am an anomaly to them. They watch me from their recliners, from under their blankets and unkempt hair. I am surely annoying them but they manage to smile politely and ignore me like a pesky child. Being the only one manic in a room is like being the only one drinking at a party.

On the unit, the patient phones, of which there are two, are mounted side by side on the wall and are answered by the patients. At least, that is, if any of them have themselves together enough to do so. I, of course, have myself extremely obnoxiously together and therefore I answer it at every opportunity.

I snatch up the phone each time it rings with the speed of a striking cobra. Picture Sponge Bob grinning with eyes wide and shining, pupils dilated, biting his bottom lip with anticipation. It rings again. I yank the receiver from its cradle wanting so badly to answer it, "Boob hatch."

Not normally being a complete dick I should know better than this, but at the moment my sensitivity is nowhere to be found. It is lying down on the job somewhere. Thank God at the last minute it pokes its head out of a broom closet and reminds me that this would most likely be offensive to both the caller and the patient they are trying to reach. All right. Geez. People should have a sense a humor.

"Hullo," I say brightly congratulating myself for showing such magnificent restraint.

"Dave! You have a phone call!"

"Valerie! Phone!"

"Mike!"

"Leslie! Phone call!" I have become the unit secretary.

Then at last, "Hey, Hon," comes Faith's voice on the other end of the line. Hot dog! A phone call for me!

"Hey!" I gush back.

"How are things? How are you feeling?"

"Great! Fabulous!" I reply. "Ready to come home."

"Really?" Faith says skeptically.

"Yep. I feel like a million bucks. Maybe even two million." The lights in the unit seem especially bright this evening.

They are more pure than they have been like they've all been replaced with new bulbs. I can see the light splitting into faint rainbows as it fractures around objects. I am distracted for a moment by its beauty.

"And your doctor said you could go home?"

"Well no," I admit. "But I'm sure it will be soon. I'm really feeling much better."

This is not entirely true. I am feeling quite remarkable as long as I don't think. When I think, I remember. I remember my life, its chaos, its deadlines, its endless commitments and obligations, its need, need, need. I remember why I was brought here in the first place. Only now it's actually worse. Something I have no intention of telling my doctors if I ever want to get out of here.

It's worse because death had been the reward I was holding out for these last ten months. It was a grinding white knuckle slog most of the time but I was close to the end. I could taste the finish line.

I had counted down, three months to go, two months to go, one month to go. I was just starting my lean for the tape when I was hospitalized. Now my finish line has been taken away from me and pushed out like fifty years. It's enough to make me return to that sporting goods store and finish what I started…if I think about it. So I don't. I live strictly in the moment. And in this moment I feel, as I've said, quite remarkable.

"Ahhh," Faith says. "Well that's great. I'm glad you're feeling better."

"Mmmm…hmmm." I am sort of lunging from one foot to

the other. It was part of a workout I once saw American speed skater Eric Heiden doing. He had crazy-big quads. She goes on to tell me she will not be able to come and see me tonight because she is too busy. I am unfazed. Nothing touches me up here in the clouds. Instead I babble on about what I did today, which is nothing and yet I expound on it like it was so marvelous it should have been covered by CNN.

"I saw a butterfly outside the window! I think it was a monarch. It flew to the very top of the building! That's very impressive, don't you think? For a butterfly, I mean. What is this building, like nine stories? Oh it's only eight? Yes, yes well still very impressive by my reckoning. And there was this car I saw from one of the windows that caught the sun just so! It was the most astounding shade of red you've ever seen in your life! I'm not kidding. It just took my breath away. You really should have seen this red!" And on and on and on. Periodically she has to tell me to slow down because she can't understand me.

I stand up one of the two chairs that sit beneath the wall phones. They have been placed there for people to sit on while talking, people less agile and less creative than myself, who don't see the chairs' potential as pieces of playground equipment. Yes. I like being up higher. It suits me. Now I resume my speed skating work out standing on the seat of the chair babbling all the while.

I consider the arms of the chair, judging the additional height they could offer me. Before I can climb onto them, the charge nurse spies me and gives me a look that says he's not up for any antics tonight. He makes a chopping motion with his hand indicating that I need to get down. I comply and do not hold it against him. Like a benevolent king, I bestow upon him my pardon.

He couldn't care less.

Faith is talking on the other end of the line. I am puzzled. It seems that I have asked her a question to which she is now responding, though for the life of me, I can't remember what it was. Neither apparently, can I follow along with her long enough to figure it out. Instead, my mind wanders off to entertain itself, checking in every so often in case a response is needed.

That's how it is when my mind gets going this fast. I can talk circles around anyone but I can't listen my way out of a paper bag. In mania's early stages this is not a problem. Not only can I still listen but I find everyone utterly fascinating. It's part of what draws people in. They know I am listening to them. They know I am hearing them. And I am, with rapt attention.

Tell me about your kids. They're wonderful! Tell me about your job. It's spellbinding! Tell me about your collection of buttons. I'm mesmerized! Tell me about your harebrained scheme to start your own alpaca ranch. It's brilliant! It'll totally work! At the moment, however, I am well past this point.

I receive one other phone call this night, one from my stepson. The outcome is just the same. I jabber on, half listening, retaining nothing and all the while amusing myself by wrapping up in the phone cord and then unwinding myself like a spinning top.

Tonight I take my first dose of Seroquel. Seroquel belongs to a class of medications known as atypical antipsychotics. I am not psychotic per say, but it is also used to treat acute mania which, according to my doctors, is where I'm headed if I'm not already there.

Doctors don't know everything though. They think seeing the sun after being held prisoner in a dark basement for months is a problem. To feel nothing for so long and then suddenly feel everything with so much intensity. Life has not only captured my interest again but my complete fascination as well.

I know I'm going a bit too fast but I can handle it. It's just that I have ten months' worth of living that has been bottled up inside me and it's all starting to come out in a rush. That's why it seems a little disorganized. But why would I want to medicate this feeling away? Why should I allow anyone to clip my wings just when I'm taking flight? Who knows what I can accomplish.

It's very important that I sleep tonight they tell me as I swallow back my lithium and Seroquel. The Seroquel should help with that, they add. The sleep, that is. For most people it's extremely sedating. But I am not interested in sleep. I am a famous writer and it is imperative that I continue my work. Don't these people know who I am?

I remain in the day room journaling again long after everyone else has gone to bed. My nurse for the night, Mari-amma, is frustrated with me. She wants me to sleep and is confounded by my energy and alertness after two days without sleep. I talk with her about nursing and family and psych meds and anything else I can get her interested in. My hunger to talk is ravenous.

I talk so fast that my words begin to tumble over each other in their rush to get out. My mind pushes them out in such a hurry that it can't always bother to line them up in the correct order. Mariamma frowns at me in confusion. I realize what is happening but I don't have time to go back and rearrange the words for her. I can't slow down because the next idea is already on the last one's heels.

Sometimes I have to skip over words or entire portions of sentences so that I can catch back up with my thoughts. If I don't, I will fall too far behind. I will lose the ideas that I am mentally formulating in front because I'm still verbally trying to communicate the ideas in back. My speech therefore, at times, is only a little better than gibberish but I don't care. I understand perfectly well what I'm saying. Mariamma will just have to keep up on her own. There's nothing wrong with me. It's the cumbersome constraints of human language that's the problem.

Eventually, the Seroquel starts to cross my eyes and I allow Mariamma to shoo me off to bed. Once again it is past midnight. I don't go to bed immediately though. I fight it. This is a little embarrassing to admit, but anyone who has ever felt the seductive lure of mania will understand. It is not easy to give up.

Mania grants the manic almost limitless energy, a wonderful feeling of euphoria, increased self-esteem, and the certainty that we can do anything. It fills our heads with a thousand dreams and an endless fountain of enthusiasm with which to pursue them. It feels so good that we don't even notice the price it's extracting from us.

If we did notice, we would see what mania claims in return includes, but is not limited to, our tact, our insight, our ability to focus, our ability to manage our finances and of course, our better judgment. No doubt, mania can feel wonderful in light to moderate doses but ultimately it cannot be controlled.

When mania goes unchecked it will feed itself like a storm gathering strength. And like all powerful storms it will leave a trail of destruction in its path. The larger the storm, the larger the devastation. I am grateful that my own manias, or hypomanias, have been mild.

Hypomania is a less intense form of mania often associated with bipolar II. Those that I have experienced have left me at times with bills for some ridiculous and inexplicable crap. They have often left me mortified by my behavior and have led me to risk my life more than a few times. Still, thankfully they have not left my life in a complete shambles the way that the full on manias of bipolar I can. I have never blown my entire retirement nest egg on magic beans. I have never run naked down Main Street or told my boss to go fuck himself and quit my job to become a traveling minstrel. I have never been taught the really hard lessons.

Tonight, though, I am not thinking of the price. I know that my current and glorious mood was triggered by two factors, an antidepressant and a lack of sleep. The antidepressant has already been removed and now I have been sent to bed. Plus I'm now gorked to my gills in mood stabilizing drugs. My budding mania's fate has probably already been sealed. Still, I wish I could ride the wave a little bit longer, milk it. It has been such a long time since I felt happiness.

Lack of sleep can trigger a manic episode. It is why bipolars have to be so vigilant to get enough rest. It is such a reliable trigger that at one time, it was even used by some psychiatrists working in mental institutions as a diagnostic tool.

In order to find out if a patient had bipolar disorder rather than some other mental illness, a psychiatrist might order the nurses to keep the patient up all night. After a night or maybe two of this, the patient would either devolve into a stumbling zombie or they would be wired up like they had just snorted half a dozen lines of coke. If it was the latter, they had themselves a diagnosis of bipolar disorder, or what was then called manic depression.

Psychiatry has made a few advances in diagnostic techniques since then. Still, knowing this about my disorder makes the solution to my problem an obvious one. To keep on feeling good, I have to avoid sleep like it is a hive of Africanized bees.

This is a terrible idea. Did I mention the fact that mania cannot be controlled? It cannot be managed or manipulated to get you to the perfect high. It has no volume control. It is an on/ off switch and once it is switched on, you never know what you're going to get. But again with the judgment thing.

I am already in the hospital on a locked psych unit and I want out as soon as possible. If they are not going to let me die, then I need to get back to the business of living. Life requires a great deal of attention and upkeep. Right now, mine is getting away from me. Each day I spend in here I fall a little farther behind.

Absurdly, however, it does not occur to me that there is no way in hell they will discharge me if I am manic. Part of the problem is that a manic mind can never determine with any accuracy just how manic it actually is…if it can recognize that it is manic at all. Also because my experience with mania has been limited more to hypomanias, I have never developed the healthy fear of mania that it deserves. In the moment, which is where all manics live, and with my concept of consequences dissolving by the day, I just want to feel good, so I pace.

Tonight, I have almost superhuman stamina thanks to whatever the hell is going on with my brain chemistry so I pit that stamina against the Seroquel. Seroquel is the enemy trying to put me to sleep. Back and forth in front of my window I go. I imagine that I am a climber in a storm on Everest. If I fall asleep, I will freeze to death. I will not sleep.

I don't feel like a climber on Everest though. I feel like a rhino hit with a tranquilizer dart by a man in a helicopter. Soon I lose the ability to focus my eyes. Seriously. I try again and again. They pass through the point of focus but can't get hold of it. Man, this stuff is strong.

Mariamma comes in and scolds me for being out of bed. I can't fight this. It's too much. I give in and get into bed. Seroquel takes this round and I resolve to let it. Who cares anyway? Thirty seconds later, I'm asleep.

Mania is no chump though. It's not going to just roll over

without a fight. It only permits a fitful sleep and pries my eyes open at each bed check. At what must be around or just after 3:00 a.m. it's had enough of sleep all together and regains the upper hand. It pesters me awake with a jittery alertness and a buzzing in my head. Any more sleep now is out of the question whether I want it or not.

I lay awake in the dark fidgeting. I jiggle my foot beneath the covers. It makes a very satisfactory rustling sort of a noise. I am pleased by this. The noise reminds me of someone beat-boxing.

It sounds nothing like someone beat boxing.

I try to jiggle a tune. Not bad, I think. I get up and go for a pee, less because I need to and more for something to do. On returning, I leap into bed landing on my back like a stunt man onto an air bag. The bed makes a worrisome cracking noise and I remind myself not to do that again. I am after all a grown man.

Next I hold my legs up in the air inspecting my feet for I don't know what, but it seems like something that maybe I should do from time to time and seeing as I have a little extra time on my hands. Hmmm. No change. The legs of my pajama bottoms slide up my legs and expose my pale ankles. Also unchanged I note. I roll off the bed and go and look out the window. Quite interesting. Back to bed. Lay on my right side. Lay on my left side. Lay on my back. This is how it goes for the rest of the night.

I have mentioned the bed checks which are done during the night for each patient on the psych floor. Policy at this hospital requires checks every 15 minutes. This is probably a bit excessive and even unrealistic during times of high census. I don't remember being checked on that often when I was depressed. In my estimation, the real world rule of thumb is probably more like 30-minute checks unless there is a good reason to do them more often.

In my case there is a good reason. I have been on every 15-minute checks without fail now because I have bipolar disorder and have not been sleeping. They are trying to rein in my out of control moods before I wind up in a full blown psychotic mania.

Every 15 minutes, my door swings silently open. Mariamma slips in and shines a flash light my way. Every 15 minutes, I wave at her. I think she hates me. I would hate me. I consider leaving the light on for her so at least she doesn't have to use her flashlight but I don't do it. The chance that I may doze off again is remote but it's not impossible. It would mean a lot to Mariamma. I try…but I can't.

The checks are my only way to tell time. Alarm clocks are not allowed in the rooms. This is because we could, you guessed it, kill ourselves with them. Perhaps we would hang ourselves with the electrical cord or break the clock and use the sharp edge of one of the broken pieces to slice open our arteries.

This may sound insane but keep in mind who we are talking about. We are, as you will remember, mental patients. And if you're thinking, well, sure but that's still a bit excessive, isn't it? Yes, it is. But the disturbing truth is that every policy here is in place because someone, somewhere, sometime before did, in fact, do it. And if you think that not allowing clocks in the patient rooms is excessive, simply pick up any of the magazines in the day room and watch all the pages fall out. The staples have all been removed from the bindings. Yep, for the cutters.

In lieu of a proper clock, it is the checks then that I use to mark the passage of time. Lying here is driving me a little bats but each check brings me, thank God, 15 minutes closer to sun up. In time though Mariamma gives up on me. She knows I'm not going to sleep any more tonight and apparently gets tired of checking on me every 15 minutes only to have me wave at her.

As sunrise approaches she eases up on the 15-minute thing. First she drops to what must be every 30 minutes and then stops checking all together. For someone like myself who is using the checks as stepping stones to daybreak, this is maddening.

I lay there in the dark with my mind racing and my feet jiggling. I have no idea how long it's been since the last check but it seems like hours. I want to lean out of my door and shout, what's a guy gotta do around here to get some checks!

Unable to wait any longer, I get up and take a shower. I dress and head down to the nurses' station to request an information printout on Seroquel. When I arrive I am pleased to discover that it is 6:00 a.m. I've made it! I have less than three hours of sleep under my belt and it feels like I just drank a double espresso.

# Chapter 39

# Fracturing

**Tuesday 10/8/2013**—The human body, I've discovered, requires a staggering amount of maintenance. If you are not aware of this, you have only to spend a week in the hospital for this point to be driven home. I was so depressed on admission that I was already behind on my personal hygiene. Depression will do that to you. It's all just too much trouble. With that as my starting point and now almost another week adrift, I am starting to get pretty shaggy.

My nails need clipping, my eyebrows need trimming, I have nearly a full-on beard, and I could grow nose hair competitively. If you saw me today, you'd think my plane had crashed and I'd just walked out of the Andes. I am, however, at least clean and showered. I find it comforting to stand under a hot spray of water so am never too ill to shower. Still, not all of us here have enough zip on the ball to manage much hygiene, or in the case of some, to even realize they need to.

As I wait for breakfast in the day room, I am able to smell the soap on my own skin and am feeling pretty dashing. I watch the other patients shuffling in. For the first time I realize that each of has our own uniform. Mine, of course, consists of my filthy striped pajama bottoms, non-skid hospital footies, T-shirt, and green corduroy coat.

Next there's Scott, "Pack Man." His uniform consists of a pair of jeans, a Green Bay Packers T-shirt, Green Bay Packers jacket, and Green Bay Packers ball cap. He likes the Pack. Scott has medication resistant depression but he has never given in. Despite multiple hospitalizations he has struggled back to his feet time and again to give life another shot. His spirit and determination are as inspiring as they are incomprehensible to the rest of us.

There's Len who wears a dirty red T-shirt, black shorts, and hospital footies. Len is a twice homeless man trying to survive the grief of losing his daughter in an auto accident. He sleeps like 18 hours a day but after what he's been through, staying conscious for six hours a day sounds like a task to rival Odysseus's voyage home to Ithaca. My hat's off to him.

There's another guy, Brent, whose uniform consists of a pair of brown cotton pants with pinstripes, clunky black dress shoes (laces removed of course), and a navy argyle sweater. Brent is a gifted musician and artist. Like Gwen, he is my friend, now that my memory allows me to have them again. Brent's anxiety around anymore than a few people is so acute that he was living the life of a shut-in prior to his hospitalization.

And on and on. Each patient has a story and a uniform that they have been wearing more or less exclusively since their admission. The women fare better than the men in this respect. They are no less impaired than the male patients but it seems they, or whoever packed for them, had the forethought to include at least a couple of outfits. They also have retained just enough concern for their appearance to bother alternating the few clothes they do have if not enough to actually bathe.

Breakfast comes and goes. It is the best meal of the day by far. The hospital food here is not what could be called five-star. Fortunately most of the psych patients are too depressed to notice. In a deep depression everything is flavorless anyway. My favorite part of breakfast is the coffee. Of course it is decaf, but what the hell. It is warm and comforting and I always save it for last.

When I return my empty tray to the food services cart, I hold back for the coffee. I head for my spot on a couch by the windows which has become as personalized as my uniform, and sit there with my feet curled under me and slowly sip, taking my time and letting the rising steam warm my face.

As the other patients finish their own breakfasts they, like me, drift away from the tables and settle themselves into recliners and armchairs. The doctors begin coming around with their residents, medical students, and physician's assistants in tow to see how we all are today. They find their patients, one at a time, take us aside to a table, and begin the morning's interrogation. How are you feeling today? How did you sleep? Any thoughts of harming yourself? Etc.

My medical team has been impressive. They have proven themselves caring and compassionate, handling me kindly and without judgment during the past week. For this reason, I am disappointed today to find that several of my team's key players have changed.

Dr. Phillips, the tall doctor with the sad green eyes who got me off the antidepressants yesterday will, thank God, continue to be my attending physician, but the rest of my team is gone. I have a new bunch who I will be dealing with starting today. I cannot help but feel that I have done something wrong and search my mind for where I may have failed.

I recall the day before when I saw my doctors. I had complimented the leading psychiatrist telling her how pretty she looked. It just came out. I also joked with her more than on the previous days making her laugh. When I am manic nearly every woman looks pretty and the pretty ones more so. I didn't mean to be flirtatious but it would not be the first time I have made that mistake. Hypersexuality is a symptom of mania and can be one of the more troublesome ones.

I wonder if the decision was made to make the change because they feared I might be developing a sexual interest in my former doctor. It may be far-fetched but in my current state of mind, it seems entirely plausible. After all it is all about me, right? What other possible reason could it be? Regardless, I feel like a ball player with a slumping batting average who has just been traded.

My new team is headed up by Dr. Lilian Martinez,

a statuesque beauty with long black hair and an olive complexion. Unlike the other doctors I have met here, psychiatry seems an unlikely choice for Dr. Martinez. Each day she comes walking onto the unit dressed to the nines. Her demeanor is always cool and detached. With her I really feel the gulf that separates me, at the moment, from the mentally healthy. I see her more as a surgeon, someone who does their best work when the patient is unconscious.

When I am cut from the herd this morning and corralled to talk with Dr. Martinez and her throng of underlings, I feel nervous and wary. I sit wriggling in my chair while she peers distastefully at me. I try my best to appear normal for her but my mind is spitting and buzzing like a live wire. My ability to focus is completely shot. If she asks me a simple question, not too many words, yes/no answer required, I can follow it. Any more than this is too much.

She explains a number of things to me and although I nod at all the appropriate times, I have absolutely no idea what she is saying. When I answer her my responses are so rambling and incoherent that she all but rolls her eyes at me. I am jabbering on like I don't know she couldn't give a rip about anything I'm saying. I can tell I am going too fast but the words just keep pouring out of me. I want to clamp my hand over my mouth. I'm giving myself away. I'll never get out of here at this rate but it's the best I can do.

I tell her I'm ready to go home and that I can work now. This is laughable and everyone can see it but me. My speech is so fast that it's nearly incomprehensible, I'm rocking back and forth non-stop, and I can't follow a thing anyone says to me. Dr. Martinez tells me she is going to double my dose of Seroquel and ignores my request for discharge. She is not pleased with me. She scribbles a few notes on her clipboard and dismisses me. Ahhh, well, so much for that.

Throughout the day I discover that my moods are all over the map. I am still happy and talkative so I engage my friends eagerly in conversation, but to my embarrassment, find myself on the verge of tears at the drop of a hat. I don't understand what is wrong with me. In the business, they call this a labile mood, meaning a mood that changes rapidly, even instantaneously and often. The Seroquel is trying to work and I now have active symptoms of both depression and mania existing simultaneously in me. Basically, my brain chemistry is completely scrambled.

Because I cannot manage to keep from losing my shit every time I start talking about something, I decide to isolate myself in a chair in the corner of the day room. I would go to my room but I am still restricted to the day room for the finger gnawing business. I have to stay where the nurses can see me. Whenever I am not in group this is where I stay rocking and writing. I still believe that I am an award-winning author but my thoughts are so scattered that the writing is now difficult. It is not flowing like before.

Jason, the therapist who led the train wreck of a couples' therapy session with Faith and me a few days ago spots me just before dinner huddled in my chair and comes over. He takes a seat next to me and asks if I have a few minutes to chat. I say that I do and am happy for the company. I am still feeling very social and don't, at the moment, recognize the potential for this to go south. I apologize for my rambling and rapid speech and explain about the Zoloft. He shrugs like it's no big deal and I am grateful. We talk at first in harmless generalities. In time though, he steers our conversation to personal matters. He is a professional and knows where a person's weak spots are. Like a Luftwaffe ace, he wings over and takes practiced aim at mine.

Why do psychiatric professionals think this is going to help anything? In my current state, I don't want anyone within a mile of my weak spots but Jason doesn't relent and under his merciless scrutiny, I crumble. For the third or fourth time that day my eyes well up, my voice cracks, and I am humiliated. He meant well and I genuinely like Jason but after a day like today, I've just had enough of falling apart in public. Until this passes, I wish he and everybody else would keep their distance.

Faith comes to see me that night and we have a wonderful visit. We sit together on the couch and she leans into me while I hold her. Apart from the setting, it's all so normal I'm reminded that I'm not always such a basketcase. It is a comforting and much needed reminder. She asks me to sing to her and there is enough mania remaining in me that I don't even feel self-conscious. We sing and giggle and cuddle like two young lovers and come 8:00 p.m. I am sorry to see her go.

That night my Seroquel is doubled in strength. I swallow the pills with a cup of water and trundle off to my room. By the time I have finished getting ready for bed, my eyelids are already heavy. I slide into bed, snap off the light, and wait for sleep. Although Seroquel is classified as an atypical antipsychotic medication, I will very soon come to believe that psychotic medication is a more apt description, at least at this higher strength. Almost as soon as I close my eyes the nightmare begins.

First, it is the voices. I don't hear them in my head. I hear them in my room. People talking all around me, not about me or to me, just in the same room with me. I think to myself, I wish these people could find a better place to meet than in a patient's room, especially one in which there is a patient trying to sleep. Can they not see me lying here in the bed?

Inexplicably there is now a judge's table in my room with a panel of judges sitting at it. I have no idea why they are there or what precisely they are judging. I just wish they would judge it somewhere else.

Then my mother is there. She is chatting with someone about God knows what. This is the only pleasant part of the experience. I have not heard my mother's voice since before she died on an operating room table in Houston more than five years ago. I want to get up and go to her but the meds are making it near impossible to even lift my head from the pillow. It is enough though to know that she is there.

I sort of need to pee though and decide that dragging myself out of bed now will be better than later. This Seroquel is kicking my ass already and it's only going to get worse. In another hour, I may be so out of it that I wet myself. I get up and go into the bathroom. I turn on the light and close the door. I look at my eyes in the mirror over the sink and realize to my surprise that I am still in bed. I have not moved. Damn.

I struggle to a sitting position, swing my feet over the side, and sit on the edge of the bed. I rub my eyes and try with a herculean effort to clear the fog from my brain. I heave myself to my feet and stumble into the bathroom. I turn on the light and close the door. Deja vu. I am determined to pee. I look at my reflection in the mirror, this time for real, and realize in frustration that I am still in bed. Awww for fuck's sake. I give up on peeing.

It is at this point that the worms living inside of my body begin to wriggle. I cannot lay still. There is a sickening tickle or itch coming from inside of me that I cannot scratch. It is most noticeable across the tops of my feet and the front of my ankles as well as across the tops of my hands and backs of my wrists. It is so awful that I want to cut off my hands and feet and blow torch the stumps.

I am squirming around in the bed in utter misery. If I move, especially if I flex or stretch my ankles and wrists, the sensation downgrades briefly to just unpleasant. If, however, I lie still for even a few seconds it becomes unbearable.

Mariamma, who is my nurse again tonight comes in several times and finds me coming out of my skin. She thinks I am having trouble sleeping and encourages me to take an Ambien, a sleep aid, that my doctors have ordered for me on an as needed basis but I firmly refuse. I am already more than drowsy enough to fall asleep but the worms inside my body won't let me lie still. If I could remain in one position for 10 seconds I'm certain I would be unconscious. But I cannot explain this to Mariamma.

I am having the bad trip of bad trips and am so unthinkably miserable that the last thing I want to do is put more drugs in my body. What I want is to say, "To hell with this. Put me on dialysis right now and remove every pharmaceutical substance you have put in me. When you've done it, discharge me from the hospital and do it *tout suite*, sister." I don't say this of course. What I in fact do—eventually—grudgingly is take the goddamn Ambien and fall asleep at last.

# Chapter 40

# Denied Again

**Wednesday 10/9/2013**—When I see Dr. Martinez and the gang that morning I tell them about my terrible experience with the Seroquel worms.

"What you're describing is called akathisia," Dr. Martinez explains. "An inability to remain still and, yes, it's very unpleasant."

I wonder if she has ever felt it herself. I doubt it.

"It's a side effect we see sometimes with antipsychotics."

Later when I am home again, I will read up on akathisia. Wikipedia defines it as a syndrome characterized by unpleasant sensations of inner restlessness that manifests itself with an inability to sit still or remain motionless. Yeah. More or less, but it loses something in the translation.

In order to address my complaints, Dr. Martinez cuts my dose of Seroquel back to the original dose, the one I tolerated before. She also adds another, a beta blocker, on an as-needed basis to reduce that inner crawling sensation and any similar side effects. Beta blockers have been traditionally used to treat heart and blood pressure issues but at lower doses have also proven effective at minimizing certain medication side effects like tremors and thankfully akathisia.

I sigh. My medication list is growing. Next she asks me about my level of depression, hopelessness, suicidal ideation, and ability to concentrate. Against my better judgment, I answer honestly and admit that I am, in all these respects, a dismal failure. It seems that despite my recent trip into the stratosphere, my depression never really went away. It was simply covered up by the mania. Now my mania is fast evaporating like an August rain shower off a hot sidewalk and I feel again the depression that's been there all year long.

As I answer her questions, I do my level best to keep from becoming emotional. I am just so discouraged though. All this trouble everyone has gone to and I'm still a wreck. I should have just stuck with my original plan to put a gun to my head on the 26th. Fuck.

My composure cracks and she sees it. My moods and have always tended to drift to extremes. That's just bipolar disorder, I guess, but now they're whip-sawing all over the place. I feel so out of control.

I take a deep breath and try to master my mutinous emotions. This part is for me one of the most embarrassing aspects of this whole disastrous hospitalization. The "fetaling" will be unpleasant to read about in my medical record one day but I will never have any personal recollection of it. This ridiculous emotional instability, I am only too frustratingly aware of.

Dr. Martinez says the difficulty I am having controlling my emotions is common and not unexpected considering that I went from very profoundly depressed on admission to manic and am now coming slamming back down again. It has been too many extremes in too brief a period of time. I am fragile and my mind needs to stabilize. Discharge denied. No surprise.

The rest of the day passes uneventfully. I am getting a little too used to the routine here, starting to feel like a fixture. I know all the shifts of all the nurses and techs and, thanks to a few days of mania, most all their stories. Today I have it together enough to realize that I am not ready to go back to work but I would still give anything to be able to finish my recovery at home in private. The people here have seen me curled up in a ball barely able to speak, trying to gnaw off my finger, standing in chairs talking a mile a minute, and choking up at the drop of a hat. I hope to God in the years to come I never run into any of them in Kroger.

The feeling of worms wriggling and tickling me from the inside is not nearly as intense as it was last night but it's not completely gone either. I put up with it as long as I can, then finally, later in the afternoon, request the beta blocker Dr. Martinez ordered. To my very great relief, it helps.

My mood remains labile so like yesterday I keep myself as isolated as I can in a day room full of other patients. When I do visit with friends or have to speak in group, I am vigilant and am able to reduce my displays of emotion to a mere few. Not bad. Baby steps.

Faith comes to visit me that night again. She looks

beautiful. We retire to our couch and begin to chat quietly. The visit, however, could not go more differently from last night. Faith, it seems, is in a foul mood. She is spoiling for a fight and I am doing everything I can to not give it to her. Her brows remain creased throughout the visit and I am unsure why she has come to see me at all if she is so irritable. She is determined, even hell bent, on discussing all our most argumentative topics especially my daughter and ex-wife. Yikes.

I steer the conversation away from these dangerous waters again and again but stubbornly she brings it back each time. I sigh and eventually have to suggest that we cut the visit short tonight. I speak in a soft and what I hope is a calming voice as if she is wearing a belt of dynamite and has an itchy trigger finger.

Emotionally I am spent to the quick and I just don't have the heart for a fight. When she leaves, she stands well away from me and informs me scowling that she will not be coming tomorrow. They buzz her out and she is gone, no kiss, no I love you. Nice.

I return to my arm chair in the day room weary and beaten. I feel lower than I have since admission. This whole hospitalization has been a waste of time. I feel no more connection to life now than I did before. Though I am a believer in reincarnation, I not only want to release this life but I don't want to come back either. Not ever. I'll stay an angel or nothing…whatever. Just no more life. Please. I sit there huddled in my green corduroy coat and wait for my evening meds so I can go to bed.

# Chapter 41

# The Return

**Thursday 10/10/2013**—When I wake up Thursday morning, I am not alone. Depression, my lifelong companion, is with me once again, heavy and oppressive. It is no longer still grappling with a fading mania the way it was yesterday. It has emerged the victor. Now unopposed, it has settled again into my bones and is squeezing my chest. I sit on the side of the bed with a lump in my throat unable to move for twenty minutes before I gather the resolve to stand.

I shower, dress, and trudge out to the day room for breakfast. Today I greet no one and keep my eyes on the floor. I am certain that people think I am a total flake, antisocial, then obnoxiously social, then antisocial again. Everyone will begin to avoid me now. I've seen it before. They think people like me are too moody, too unpredictable. So what. All the better. I've lost my appetite for small talk anyway or any of the general niceties required for maintaining friendships. Don't ask anything of me because I have nothing inside to give. It was all just a trick of the mania. I'm sorry if I made you believe there was more. It is the ugly truth of me and I can no more prevent this than I can prevent the changing of the seasons.

I sit alone with my back to the rest of the day room and my shoulders hunched. I neither read nor write. I see no point in it. The fact that I am not a famous writer has at last sunken in. It is both disappointing, like waking up after dreaming you were a millionaire, and embarrassing. How could I ever have believed such a thing? I've never even written a story, let alone a best-selling novel. How could I not have seen it was the mania? Yet again, I feel like an idiot. It humbles me, makes me wonder how I can ever tell what is real.

I feel like every time I blink I turn into a different person. Each time I think I know who I am, the ground shifts away from underneath me. All my interests, life plans, and priorities disappear overnight. I look around and feel like I have been living someone else's life. None of it matters. I'm nothing like that guy. I'm this other guy. I shift everything around in my life and in my head to suit the new me...the "real" me only to have it happen all over again...and again.

I decide I am through being fooled. From here out I will fool everybody else. I don't know if I will ever take my own life or not but I want the freedom to choose. I know that in order to have that choice I first have to get the hell out of here. When the gang comes around to deliver my daily brow beating, I am flawless. Yes, ma'am, I slept well. No, ma'am, I am not feeling depressed at all. No, ma'am, I have no thoughts of hurting myself. I am really doing much better, thank you.

If I was my doctor, I would discharge me on the spot. This is not however, the case. They want to hold me a little longer and make sure that I'm not going to shoot off into the clouds again or plunge back into the dumps. A little late for that one. I numbly plod through my routine of groups and meal times and medication administrations. I have no interest in journaling seeing as I have no book deal in the works, but I do read a little on and off. It gets me off the unit for a while even if it's only in my mind.

Dr. Phillips comes to see me that afternoon and asks how things are going. I cannot lie to this woman. Something about her eyes, I think. It's like her super power. When she looks at me I can really tell she cares about me and it just breaks down the walls. Who can lie to someone who truly cares about them?

I admit to her that I am feeling low and discouraged. And once I get started I begin to pick up speed. I explain to her that I have wasted more than a week of my life in here. That I came in depressed and despite all the meds and restrictions and therapy, I am still depressed. That despite my depression, it appears that I am chiefly being medicated for mania, a condition that I was not even experiencing prior to my admission. That I feel as hopeless as ever if not more. That my lithium makes me dizzy and no one will believe me. That my Seroquel makes me squirm, and on and on I go. So much for fooling folks.

Dr. Phillips listens intently and addresses all of my

concerns. Mostly, she explains that these things take time. A typical doctor's response, yet it still carries more weight somehow when she says it. And when she leaves I always feel like she has heard me.

Sometime before dinner, one of the other patients, Leah, a young red head suffering with depression, approaches the piano. She opens the seat and sifts through the handful of loose copies of sheet music inside. Unable to settle on any one piece, she puts the entire stack on the music stand above the keyboard. She closes the seat and sits down. Her posture is ram rod straight. She straightens her sheets and positions her fingers gently on the keys. She takes a breath, and begins.

Patients are spread out across the day room each engaged in one activity or another. Most are in recliners watching one of the two TVs. A few are working the puzzles. Two are playing Monopoly, one is reading, and I am staring lifelessly at nothing. For the next 15 minutes or so, however, none of us so much as breathes.

Within moments both TVs are turned off out of respect and nothing but the sound of the piano fills the room. The music is classical. I recognize it. Bach, I think, and the beauty of it raises goose bumps on my skin. She plays straight through the stack of sheets front to back despite the variety of composers or order of the sheets. She flashes it her first time through without so much as a hiccup and I believe she has no idea whatever that she holds the whole room spellbound behind her.

You never know where talent resides or through whom it

will shine. It is in the old and the young. It is in the kind and unkind, the rich and the poor. It is in prisoners and priests and, yes, it is even in mental patients. It may be suppressed at times by the patient's illness but it is never extinguished.

Leah brings that piano to life like she's not even trying and in doing so, she takes us all to a place where there is no sickness and where beauty shines like brilliant sunlight. As long as her fingers are still moving, we bask in the glow of that sunlight each of us hoping for just a little more time. When she is finished, everyone in the room applauds.

# Chapter 42

# Doldrums

**Friday**—I am awakened Friday morning by a girl from the lab. She has come to draw my lithium level. Lithium has a very narrow therapeutic range. Take too little and it doesn't do anything. Take too much and it is toxic. The doctors are hoping that I'm on the baby bear dose, just right. Lithium has been used successfully to treat bipolar disorder for more than forty years. It is a reliable medicine with a proven track record and in my case a good choice because it has been shown especially effective in reducing suicidal tendencies.

The girl drawing my blood is not the same as the one who drew it earlier in the week nor is my reaction the same to having my blood drawn. This morning I could not be less interested. I'd like to pull the covers over my head and go back to sleep. I'd like to hold the sun somehow below the horizon for just another few hours and keep the world at bay. But I can't.

When the girl from the lab finishes with me, I collapse

back onto the bed and turn away from her. As she leaves, she flips off my light on her way out and this time I do not budge. I have maybe an hour. No one gets to sleep late in here. I guess it's not healthy. The staff comes around to wake us all up, ready or not, between about 7:00 and 7:30. Still, today I'll take another hour.

After breakfast, I sit nursing my cup of decaf on the couch. My mind is kind of blank. I feel numb again. I shouldn't be surprised. Psych meds don't work overnight. Most have to build up in the system. In most cases they need two to three weeks to begin noticeably reducing symptoms. Having the Zoloft affect me the way it did was unusual. I know the lithium and Seroquel just need more time.

I have to be patient but I'm tired of being sick. Tired of being the focus of so much attention by my family and doctors. I prefer to be the one stoically standing beside the bed, not the one in it. I prefer to be the one everyone can rely on not the one everyone has to be concerned about. Of late, I have been the one everyone has to keep watch over and talk quietly around. I shake my head in disgust. I hate myself.

If there's nothing anyone can do except to wait for the meds to take hold then why can't I just wait at home. Well, okay. I guess I know why but I'm at least better now than I was on admission. I'm not in the fetal position. I know I'm not in a school for the gifted and talented.

I'm not ready to let go of the idea of suicide yet. It's my security blanket. But I'm willing to at least shelf it for the time being and give these meds another week or two…see what they can do. That's pretty responsible I'd say. Pretty fucking sane.

They keep us to a pretty tight schedule here between groups of one sort or another. It annoys me no end now that I'm feeling antisocial again. They want us to stay busy. I get that but depression just makes you want to sit and do nothing. I go to the groups anyway. I can refuse but then they might catch on to how low I still am and postpone my discharge even longer.

Finally about 4:00 in the afternoon, they leave us mercifully the hell alone to veg or work puzzles or watch TV. Whatever. I have no interest in anything but vegging anymore. I have forgotten my journal completely. What a waste of time. I stare out the window with disinterest and wonder idly what it feels like out there. I have not been outside in ten days.

Just before dinner that evening there is a fight. It's not much of a fight but it breaks up the usual routine. Donna, one of the other patients, and accepted by most to be the sickest amongst us, goes after a nurse tech about something I'm sure the tech had no control over.

Shouting is no big thing here so at first I barely look up when Donna starts in. Something about not getting her computer time. There is a computer in an office here and patients are allowed limited access to it if they sign up ahead of time. Whatever. I hate computers. Donna apparently, does not. It sounds like she wants to use it now but the office is locked and it doesn't look like it's going to be unlocked for her either. Unable to control her agitation, she lunges at the tech her arms windmilling.

The staff are quick to sniff out trouble early. They see where this is going long before it gets there and are already moving before Donna does. They aren't quite quick enough to prevent it but they're slick. Donna barely lands her first glancing blows before she is surrounded, contained, and removed from the day room. I do not see her again that night.

After dinner I curl into a corner chair near the piano. During the day, the corner is lit by natural light from the windows that form a continuous wall down this side of the day room as well as a ceiling over it, like a green house or the conservatory on the board game Clue. Because of the glass ceiling though there are no overhead lights here and as a consequence, the corner falls into forgotten shadow after dark. Perfect for me.

At night most of the patients gather near the TVs under the lights and close to the nurses' station. The sound of a nursing unit at night is almost comforting, the quiet bustle of routine. Another day drawing to a close. I am soothed by the sounds but only if I am separated from them by a distance. I prefer to be apart from others and feel at home in the dark...like a mole.

I wait for my night nurse to come on shift. It is Margaret. She is one of my favorites. I'm always impressed that she is able to show such genuine concern for her patients. I can only imagine what it must be like to listen to people moaning about their lives day after day. Avoiding burnout seems like a tall order to me but she manages to do it. Psych nurses are a special bunch. They have certainly gained my respect and gratitude during my stay here.

Margaret pulls up a chair next to mine for our evening chat. The chat is the assessment. In psych it's not about dressings and wounds and such, it's about thoughts and feelings. Ughh, a topic I'm ready to choke on. I sigh and answer her questions, trying not to let my weariness on the subject show. I give her the answers I hope a model patient ready for discharge would give her and she records them all on her clipboard.

When we are finished I ask if I can take my meds early and get some sleep. Faith is not coming so I have no reason to stay up. Margaret raises her eyebrows, it's only a little past 8:00, but she doesn't object. I follow her to the nurses' station and wait at the ubiquitous loony bin Dutch door while she retrieves my evening meds.

She returns with a tiny paper medication cup that looks like something you'd put ketchup in at Burger King and half a Styrofoam cup of water. I peer into the ketchup cup and rustle the pills around a little. I sigh and toss them back with a gulp of the water then hand the empties back.

"Thanks, Margaret. Good night," I tell her turning to head down to my room. "Have a good shift."

"Good night, Frank," she answers over my shoulder.

# Chapter 43

# Release

**Saturday and Sunday, the final days**—Saturday feels like any other day of the week. No sleeping in. No break from groups. Same routine. My emotions have finally righted themselves like a sailboat with a lead keel and I'm thankful for that. I can talk to people if I want to now without fear that I might get choked up over some idiotic triviality. I just don't really feel like it. I want to leave.

Every day since Wednesday, I have been asking my doctors if I can be discharged and every day they say no. Today is no different. Dr. Phillips does at least give me reason to hope. Today she tells me that she has Monday in mind for my date of discharge but will leave it in her notes that if the on-call doctor who covers for her tomorrow feels comfortable, she will not object to his discharging me home a day sooner. I could be down to my final 24 hours of confinement.

Another bit of good news comes my way from my day nurse. My day room restriction has been lifted. A privilege earned, no doubt, by the continued attachment of all ten of my fingers. This means I am free to spend time in my room as I wish. It doesn't change much of anything though. The therapists still find me there and drag me off to group with the same annoying regularity they did when I was in the day room.

The day passes uneventfully. I don't talk much but neither do I have any public displays of emotion. I am invisible. I am a ghost.

Not long before dinner, Faith calls to let me know she will not be coming to visit me again tonight and I am okay with it. Being alone just feels simpler right now. Our conversation is not long, yet I do let her know there is a possibility of discharge tomorrow when I see the on-call doctor. She sounds as excited as I am at the prospect of me coming home.

That night there is a *Walking Dead* marathon on TV, the very popular post-apocalyptic zombie show. Nearly everyone on the unit is glued to the big screen all night. Seems like pretty ill-advised viewing for a bunch of mental patients if you ask me. I keep waiting for one of the staff to get up and change it but no one ever does.

I don't much go in for gore so I drift over to the older TV on the other side of the day room. No one is watching it so I browse the collection of old VHS tapes and select *City of Angels* with Nicholas Cage and Meg Ryan. I power up the VCR, slip in the tape, and make myself comfortable on the floor in front of the set.

It feels good to just sort of veg out and not think about

anything. It's the first time I have watched TV since I have been here. The movie is not bad either. It's been years since I have seen it. I forgot most of it so it's all new to me. And Meg Ryan is a good bit hotter than I remember. After the movie I rewind the tape ("rewind"...hilarious) and go straight to bed.

Sunday morning, I shower, comb my hair and dress in the blue jeans I wore in the day of my admission. My pajamas are filthy and beginning to stink. There is technically a laundry room on the unit back near the quiet room, though it never once occurred to me to use it. Then again, my cognition has not exactly been what you might call stellar. But I want to look respectable today even if it's just an act. It's not completely an act though. I am better than when I came in. Maybe it is time I put some pants on.

I'm not optimistic and I still can't feel but I'm not suicidal anymore. My plans that have been swinging back and forth between living and dying feel like they've quieted. I'm going to give the medicine time to work. Until it does I realize there is no point in trying to make decisions regarding my future. I'll just put everything out of my mind. For now my only plan is to keep putting one foot in front of the other and let time pass.

After breakfast I sit alone in the day room and wait for my turn to meet with the doctor. It feels like he meets with every patient on the unit before he finally lets me know I'm up. I carry my coffee cup over to the table where he and a couple of psychiatric residents are waiting for me. There's no more than the cool dregs of coffee left at the bottom but holding onto the cup provides an odd measure of security so I hang onto it.

Over the next five to ten minutes I sit like a prisoner before a parole board and answer every question put to me. I do my best to give the doctors all the answers they want to hear. I smile at the appropriate times and maintain eye contact when I talk. When the interview ends, I finally hear the words I have been waiting for. I am to be discharged home later this morning.

I call Faith and tell her the news. She says she will be there that afternoon to get me to be sure the doctor has time to get his orders in. I hang out until then, bored but thankfully not hassled by having to attend groups. Sunday is the one day of the week that the patients are left to themselves.

I lay on my bed in my room or sit on the couch in the day room. Sometimes I pace back and forth in front of the window by the door to the unit watching for Faith. I feel like a dog at the pound waiting for its owner to come. When I look up later in the day, she is there at last. We sign the forms, my belongings are returned, I am even allowed to replace the laces in my shoes. I say goodbye to a couple of friends and then am buzzed out with Faith at my side.

We ride the elevator down to the first floor and then exit the front door of the hospital under overcast skies and into a fine drizzle. I don't mind at all. I am free.

# Chapter 44

# Re-entry

It is another ten days before I am able to return to work after my hospitalization. Faith wishes I would wait a full two weeks, but I feel I need to get back to the world if I'm going to make a go of this. My memory is not back up to speed yet, sometimes I have difficulty finding words, I still feel slightly dizzy all the time, and my hands tremble so much that it's difficult for me to draw blood or start IVs. All this is a result of the meds I am still trying to adjust to, chiefly the lithium. I'm getting by, though, and seeing Dr. Douglas again every couple of weeks.

I confess my struggles and hospitalization to both Brian and my father. It feels like a mistake but both are thankfully supportive. Brian seems to me to be torn between trying to decide if bipolar is a real thing, offering other rationalizations for what happened, and seeing how it might also explain an awful lot about the way I have been since he has known me.

My father is unfailingly kind without a trace of judgment

at all as he listens to me. It is both comforting and humiliating. Deep down I still feel I am letting him down. The years since I was a child have mellowed him and the death of my mother nearly broke him. If there is anything that defined this complicated man it is that he loved my mother with all his heart. Our shared grief over her death brought us closer together and our relationship, at long last, grew not only to that of a father and son, but also that of two old friends.

As far as the lithium goes, I find the side effects, more tolerable than those of other meds I have tried. In time, even these begin to smooth out, except for the tremors which I am learning to work around. I think I may even stay on my regime this time, maybe for good.

Lithium is not without its risks. I have to periodically have my blood drawn to monitor my kidney functions. A certain number of people are unable to tolerate lithium and can suffer permanent kidney damage from it. It's rare, but it's why doctors watch so diligently for early signs of trouble. If they see any, they stop their patient's lithium right away.

As luck would have it, I am one of these people. A couple of months in, my renal function tests begin to go sour and I am forced to give up the first medicine I thought I could stick with. Figures.

After that, Dr. Douglas and I work together to try and come up with a workable alternative to lithium. I don't like any of the suggestions she makes as I know too well about the side effects of each drug. At last she convinces me to try a medicine called Lamictal. I am skeptical because I tried it before and it killed my libido the last time. Dr. Douglas tells me that while everyone is different, it really shouldn't do that, so I reluctantly agree to give it another whirl.

When the same thing happens again I become discouraged. I am unwilling to take a medicine that negatively impacts my private life with Faith, so without telling Dr. Douglas I just stop it. While I'm at it, I decide I am sick of feeling drowsy all the time too and toss my Seroquel into the trash along with the Lamictal.

I feel like I've tried every option I'm willing to at one time or another and each one has had more cons than pros. I'd be happy to take something if there was something that didn't suck, but I've no options now. I'll just have to handle the ups and downs of bipolar. Fuck it. It's all I really know anyway.

I consider continuing to see Dr. Douglas so she can at least monitor me, but I'm too embarrassed. I don't want to try to explain this to her. She won't agree and probably won't keep me as a patient anyway. She would just say, "Why do you bother coming to see me if you're not going to do what I say." And she'd be right…so I don't try and tell her. I call and cancel my next appointment and strike, once again, out on my own. Within a month I am manic.

More than two months go by in a blur. My interests in everything explode. I'm reading everything in print. The teetering stack of books reappears on my side table. I'm cleaning the house from top to bottom, rearranging the Tupperware under the cabinets, plotting all kinds of home improvements. My thoughts are going so fast that I feel like a circus stuntman racing a motorbike around the inside of my skull. The nightly silent movies that play at triple speed on the inside of my eyelids each night are back. My hypersonic speech is back and so are all my rambling phone calls to neglected family and friends.

I can barely contain myself. There is so much kinetic energy inside me I don't know what to do. I don't feel like I'm about to explode. I feel like I already have exploded yet some force is containing the blast...not allowing it to expand. It's an irresistible pressure inside me begging for release. It's the sort of pressure that makes me yell when I should stay quiet, that makes me mash my accelerator to the floor when I should drive the speed limit, that makes me laugh uproariously when I should only chuckle. It makes me want to run crashing into the walls, to shout, to break shit, and to blast the volume on the stereo.

One morning on the way to work, I'm listening to a Beethoven symphony at a volume sure to cause hearing damage. Beethoven is my favorite when I am manic because it is the only music that feels as intense as my thoughts. I glance up as a flock of birds breaks across the sky above the road and I notice that their movements match perfectly with the music. The idea of coincidence dissolves quickly when I see that it isn't just the birds.

The entire world is syncing with Beethoven. The wind, the shimmering leaves, the snapping of flags, the movement of the traffic, the blinking of turn signals, even the flashing of sunlight through the branches of passing trees. The scope of what is happening is breathtaking. The audacity that it would take to even think about pulling something like this off, the level of direction and organization that it must require, all of it leaves no doubt in my feverish mind who is behind it...God, and he's doing especially for me.

It's brilliant because no one knows what is happening except me. God has turned the whole world into a stage and everything in it into an unwitting performer. It is His gift to me because He knows I will see it and understand. I am staggered by the spectacle of it all and grateful beyond words.

The hairs are standing up on my arms, up my neck, and over my scalp. I begin grinning and shaking my head in amazement. I look right and then left, up to the sky, and then behind me in my mirrors trying to take it all in. It's flawless, all timed down to the smallest detail to Beethoven's booming genius. God has outdone himself this morning and is enjoying seeing me in awe. I feel Him all around me effortlessly orchestrating the dance and grinning along with me.

The symphony ends, as it eventually must, but the high remains. It has been a privilege to see, a gift that has left me trembling not only physically but spiritually as well. It is the greatest performance I have ever witnessed and I know I will remember it always.

As the mania progresses, my thoughts become more disorganized. I become scattered. One day I forget to wear my shoes to work and have to call home and ask Faith to bring them to me. I clip countless pictures of water from magazines and paste them into a composition book believing that this will somehow return the water levels in the ravaged Aral Sea back to normal; restoring what was once the world's fourth largest inland body of water. Don't ask.

I buy a violin and a "statue" of a meerkat that I decide I simply must have. In one morning of furious scribbling I rough out the entire plotline to a graphic novel Brian and I have been talking about doing for years. "This time," I tell him. "We're really going to make it happen. Probably within the next six months!" I make everything seem possible and wrap Brian up in my exuberance for a while yet again. Sorry, Bri.

I decide one day that I will start an alternative medicine clinic at the university where I am working. I pour out my idea to the department head as well as one of the attending physicians, my wife and a couple of co-workers. I make plans to conduct a survey of the patients passing through my unit in order to gauge their openness to alternative therapies either in conjunction with more traditional medicine or alone when traditional medicine has failed.

Those that I pitch my idea to are unwilling to commit to anything but my energy and enthusiasm seem to impress them. I produce pages of research that I download from the Internet showing the numbers of other well-known university and research hospitals around the country that have similar programs already in place. I quote statistics and numbers and costs as if I have any clue at all about what I'm talking about.

I assume, of course, that I will be the manager of this new clinic and bring in all the new doctors and practitioners it will require. I assume the hospital will fly me, expenses paid, all over the country to visit the other centers and see how they run. And of course I assume "my" clinic will become a huge financial success for the university as well as help countless suffering patients who had previously lost hope.

To be fair, the idea is not half bad. A great many of my manic ideas aren't half bad. The problem is that I have no follow-through. It would take someone who is as driven as I only temporarily appear to be in order to carry this off. Regardless of what I might tell you, I'm not that guy. It's never going to happen.

That's what mania does. It makes commitments you can't possibly keep. It sets goals you have no hope of reaching. It establishes friendships you will never be able to maintain once the mania fades even if you wanted to...which you won't. Trust me. When the whirlwind in your mind subsides you won't give two shits about the commitments, the goals, speaking to friends, or pretty much anything at all. But you will be stuck trying to fake it all the same.

You will have to hope to God you didn't get yourself in too deep to politely slip out of your commitments. You will have to avoid the people to whom you rambled on nonsensically or hugged when you should have simply said hello. You will have to force yourself to smile at the people you can't avoid and pretend to be the same person they remember so that they don't figure out what a complete fucking psycho you are. In short, you will have to live the life of two people and make it look like one. When I'm manic, I always forget this.

There are at least a couple of bonuses to this episode

though. I reconsider my earlier assessment that this book was a waste of time. I dig out the hand written journal I kept while in the hospital and complete the bulk of a first draft of this book. And during it all, I work a crap ton of overtime and my bank account swells with the added income. Not bad. Then it's all gone and I know what's waiting for me.

I should see it coming by now but I never do. The sudden emptiness stuns me. Just like that, I have no interest in any of the things have so captivated me for months. They're all stupid. Almost overnight I go from thinking that life is take-your-breath-away beautiful and everything in it is connected and important to thinking that absolutely nothing matters. We only think things are important because someone else somewhere along the way arbitrarily decided they were. The truth is, everything…all of it, is meaningless. I shake my head in bewilderment. How could I have been so taken in…again?

Saying I'd rather deal with the ups and downs of bipolar when I'm stable or even when I'm manic is easy, but when I'm depressed…not so much. Once again I begin to puzzle over a solution, check and recheck. Were there any treatments I might have missed that could help?

I want to go back and see Dr. Douglas but she won't be pleased. I quit all my meds and dropped out of therapy without a word. I haven't been there in months. I'm a terrible patient. I'm a terrible person. What's the use anyway? If I'm no more willing to take the medicines now than I was before, then going back would just be a waste of time for both of us. In the end, though, I set the damn appointment.

What the hell.

As an established patient, I get in quickly. Dr. Douglas could lecture me but she doesn't and I am grateful. We talk about what has been going on and how to move forward from here. She assures me there are still many more medications we can try and encourages me not to give up. After talking about several she convinces me not to try something new but instead, to consider going back on Depakote, the first medicine I ever tried. She points out that it worked well for me for years and by my own admission I had no side effects from it. Hmmm. Not bad. I'll give it a go.

# Chapter 45

# Lessons Learned

For a change, I follow my doctor's suggestion. I fill the Depakote prescription and take it as directed without missing a dose. Would you believe it…it works. At least it's been working so far. No paranoia, no hallucinations, no ridiculous exuberance or dark withering depression. All of it, gone. I am currently stable and doing just fine. One medicine, once a day, no side effects. For the first time in years, I am enjoying a level of predictability in my life that I was beginning to think was impossible. Could it really be this simple? For me, at least, it appears it can.

I thought I would, in a strange way, miss my illness. After all, it was the only thing I really ever knew. Would living without my extremes be like living in a land without seasons? I mean, I could do without the crushing cold of the dead of winter and the wilting dog days of summer, but wouldn't endless mild boring days of sunshine and 72 degrees become even worse over time? I need days of quiet snowfall as much as days of backyard barbeques and swimming. I need to see the bright green new leaves of spring as much as the brilliant oranges and reds of autumn. How could I live without the variety of my ever-changing moods?

It has not, thank God, turned out to be a land without seasons. Instead, it is a land with more beautiful and temperate seasons. The winters don't freeze my pipes, and the springs don't bring tornadoes that tear my roof off. The autumns don't fill my gutters with leaves and the summers don't bring droughts that kill my lawn. It's nice.

Sometimes I find myself looking back on my behavior through the years. Times when I said too much, acted emotionally in front of co-workers, lost my temper over stupid shit, wasted countless hours on totally unrealistic pursuits, and acted just generally bat-shit crazy. Obviously a lot of that I have to own. It's just me. But how much of it was my illness? How many times did I make a fool of myself because of my out-of-control moods and how many times could I have prevented it by simply accepting and taking responsibility for what the doctors were telling me? I've kicked myself enough in my life though, so I have to let it go. Regret changes nothing.

At times I do miss the passion, drive, and creativity that came with my manias. Some nights when I look up and the moon is just the moon, I feel a pang of loneliness for the magic gone now from my life. But it's all being made up for by having a fixed identity. In my opinion, the most frustrating thing about having bipolar disorder was waking up over and over again with completely different priorities. It was like repeatedly finding I was a stranger in my own body. I was forever trying to figure out who I was. Now I think I know. I'm still stepping cautiously but I'm beginning to trust that this time I'll stay. Maybe this time I really am the "real me".

And if you think the irony is lost on me that the medicine responsible for this turnaround is the very same medicine that Dr. Howard prescribed for me back in 1998, or that more than a decade of useless struggle and embarrassment could have all been avoided if only I had taken it…it isn't. Rats.

What I've learned from the years careening around my self-constructed roller coaster of a life, among other things, is that bipolar disorder is not a black and white illness. It is expressed in endless shades of gray. Though extreme cases are often sensationalized in the news as in, "Bipolar Woman Kills Kids then Self" or "Bipolar Man Goes on Shooting Spree at Local Shopping Mall." This is an unfair portrayal that breeds fear and prejudice.

While the illness can be frightening in some cases, in others it may be so mild that it is mistaken for mere eccentricity or even quite often missed all together. To be diagnosed with bipolar disorder is not, in and of itself, cause to panic. It does not have to mean a life of crazed ups and downs or forever being controlled by the whims of wildly penduluming moods. Everyone is different.

If you have been diagnosed with bipolar disorder, it is important that you accept this new health paradigm in your life and learn to live within its generally forgiving constraints. You should do your research, find a psychiatrist you trust, avoid alcohol and/or drugs, get enough sleep, try to exercise, and above all else, take your medications as prescribed. If there is a problem with your medications, call your doctor and let the doctor make any needed changes.

Whenever possible, try not to judge yourself too harshly for abnormal behavior you may have demonstrated. What's done is done. Sometimes it just can't be helped. Every illness involves similar occasional and unavoidable slips of one's dignity. Nobody but busy bodies care about that stuff anyway.

Friends and family members of bipolars should also do their research. Learn the signs of impending illness. Help your bipolar person remember to take their medications. Faith asks me almost every night, "Did you take your meds?" I'm proud to report that I can truthfully always answer, yes. If you're unsure, however, watch the pill counts in their bottles to make sure they are being straight with you .We are famous for adjusting our own medication regimes or stopping them all together. Keep the telephone number for their psychiatrist in your own contacts list as well. Try not to become frustrated when your person becomes ill and all your advice and attempts to help them seem to go nowhere. You are trying to reason logically with someone whose brain is unwell. How can they possibly be swayed by logic when the logical part of their brain is as fried as everything else? It is foolish to expect rational responses from an irrational mind.

To all involved, join a local support group if you feel you

need a stronger network of people who understand what you're going through. They can be quite helpful and a quick Internet search should be able to turn up at least one of them meeting within a few miles of where you live. The National Alliance on Mental Illness or NAMI is a good place to start. Visit their website at www.nami.org.

And here is a last parting bit of advice to take away from this account if you take nothing else…denial is for chumps.

# Epilogue

It has been nearly two and a half since I have been healthy and stable. I continue to see Dr. Douglas for check-ups, but my appointments are brief and come only once every few months. When I was sick in 2012 the story I used to explain my hospitalization to anyone who asked was a "bout of pancreatitis." It worked pretty well so I let it stand up until now. Today, however, I decide it's time I tell Cornelia the truth.

Bipolar disorder tends to run in families. The more family members who have it, the higher the likelihood that a person will get it as well. If both parents are bipolar a child's chances of getting it too are as high as fifty percent. If, however, only one parent has the disorder the risk drops to around ten percent. Not bad odds for Cornelia, but being adopted, I have no idea what else lies in my family tree. What I do know is my biological mother was an artist and much has already been made of the connection between bipolar disorder and creativity. It makes me wonder. Either way Cornelia should know.

It is a beautiful Saturday afternoon in April so I take

Cornelia on a picnic. We grab some take-out and head over to a local city park. It is a beautiful park with a large pond that has a spraying fountain in the middle of it. The pond also has a wooden pier that juts out into it. The planks are grey and weather-worn. We decide the pier will make the perfect picnic spot and make our way out to the end of it where there are benches built into the railings on either side.

We make ourselves comfortable on one of the benches and dig into our lunches taking in the beauty of the day. The sky is that clear dark blue of spring. A jet's faint contrail is visible high overhead. The sun is warm and shimmers off the wind-rippled water. Every now and again a stray breeze catches a mist of the fountain's spray and we feel it cool on our skin. About a dozen seagulls either sit bobbing on the water or drift lazily on the wind. I love seagulls. Some birds make flight look like work. Others make it look like it requires at least the amount of effort one would expect it to. But seagulls just hang effortlessly in the sky as if the air was so solid you could walk up it like steps and join them.

"You remember that time when I had to go into the hospital for pancreatitis?' I begin.

"Uh huh," Cornelia answers and takes a sip of her drink. Her voice is wary like she always thought something seemed a little fishy about that incident.

"Well, it wasn't exactly for pancreatitis." Cornelia doesn't answer just looks out over the water and waits for the rest. She's like that. Patient. Slowly I tell her what really happened. I omit how close I came to killing myself. I avoid the word suicidal altogether and use words I hope are less frightening, like hopeless and severely depressed. Still I think she senses just how depressed a person would have to be to actually be hospitalized for it but she doesn't ask for more specifics. A dagger of guilt stabs me beneath the ribs for almost leaving her, but I ignore it and press on.

I tell her that bipolar disorder is hereditary and therefore there is a small chance she could get it too. If not her then her kids and that she should not take any signs of the illness for granted, but to let someone know. I assure her that the chance is very low indeed and it will get even lower with each generation, but still I want her to know. I want her to be smart. I wasn't. I apologize to her for not taking better care of myself because I don't know what else to say and because the dagger is still sticking in me.

She thinks on all that I have told her and I wait for her response. Finally she nods. "But you're okay now, right?" she asks.

I smile. "Yeah. I'm great." Cornelia nods again with satisfaction. It seems that is enough for her. "I found a medication that works well for me and I take it every day," I tell her.

She gives me a crooked smile. "Well, see that you do." We both laugh. The tension is broken. She looks out at the water again. "This is a nice park."

I nod. "Yeah. It really is."

## Acknowledgements

My sincerest thanks to my family, friends, and doctors. You cared for me when I could not care for myself. You accepted me, never judging, even as I judged myself so harshly. I am forever grateful for your kindness and understanding.

Printed in Great Britain
by Amazon